PRODUCE OF EUROPE

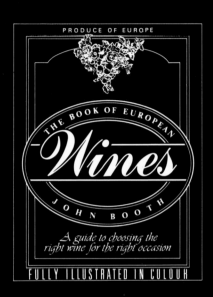

THE BOOK OF EUROPEAN

Wines

JOHN BOOTH

A guide to choosing the
right wine for the right occasion

FULLY ILLUSTRATED IN COLOUR

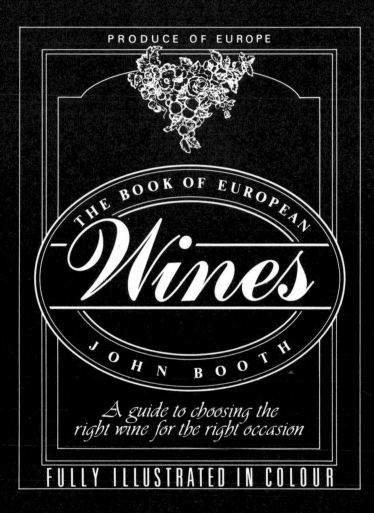

PRODUCE OF EUROPE

THE BOOK OF EUROPEAN

Wines

JOHN BOOTH

*A guide to choosing the
right wine for the right occasion*

FULLY ILLUSTRATED IN COLOUR

the
apple
press

A QUINTET BOOK

Published by Apple Press Ltd
293 Gray's Inn Road
London WC1X 8QF

ISBN 1 85076 027 6

This book was designed and produced by
Quintet Publishing Limited
6 Blundell Street, London N7

Art design by Bridgewater Associates
Editor Stephen Paul

Typeset in Great Britain by
Q.V. Typesetting Limited, London
Colour origination in Hong Kong by
Hong Kong Graphic Arts Company Limited, Hong Kong
Printed in Hong Kong by Leefung-Asco
Printers Limited

CONTENTS

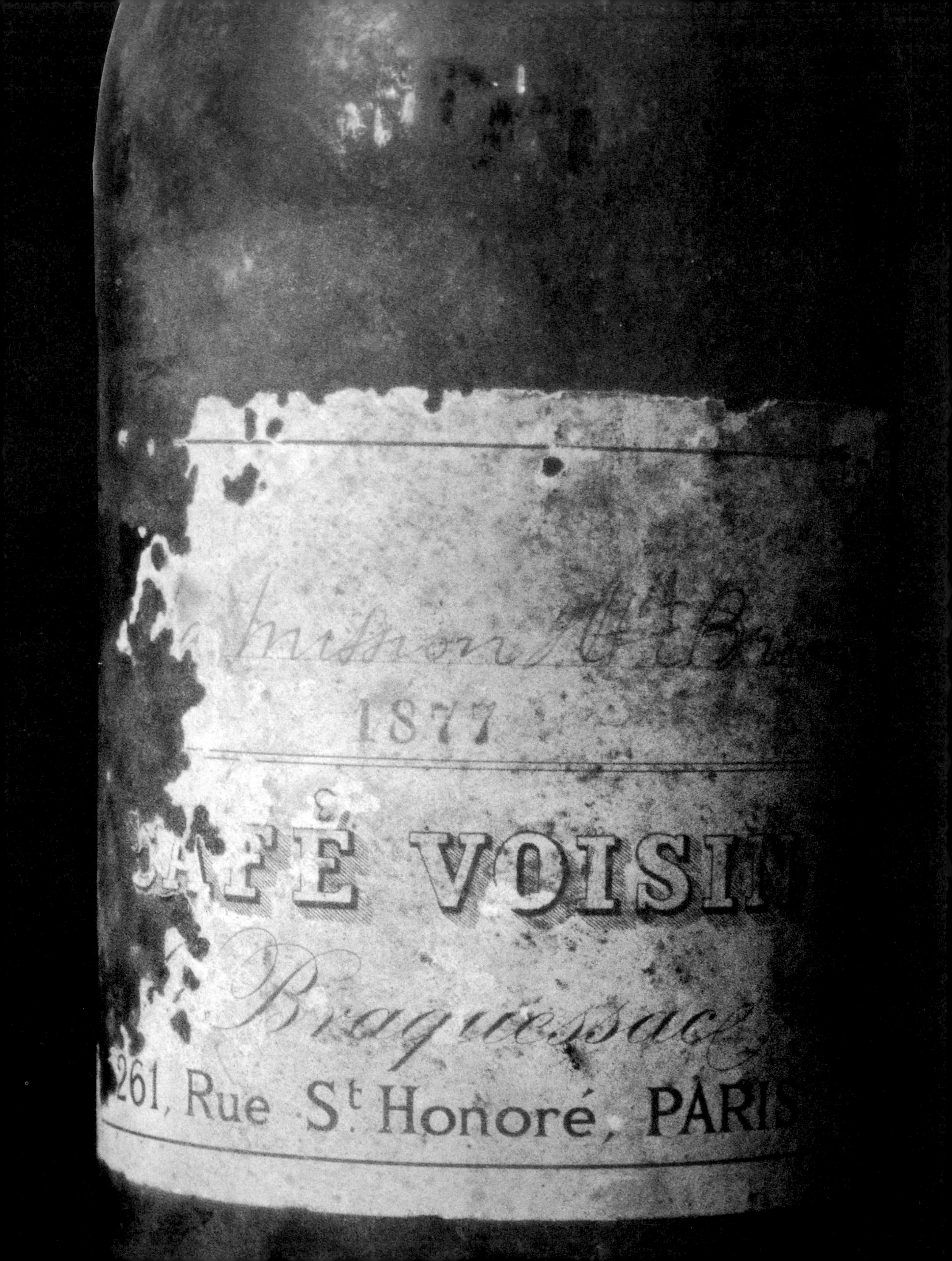

1877
AFÉ VOISIN
261, Rue St. Honoré, PARIS

HISTORY

Hieronymus Braunschweig's illustration of a pot still *(above)*, an early attempt at producing alcohol.

Even in an age of science, there is something miraculous about wine and it is easy to understand why it was associated with divinity and given god-like attributes in the civilizations of the past.

Wine is a natural phenomenon, one that could occur without the assistance of man, although the story of wine would be very different if it were left to its own devices.

The vine has been known from the beginning of history and fossilized remains have been found dating from 10 million years before the birth of Christ. *Vitis vinifera* is the father of all modern vines and is distributed in various forms in the wine growing areas of the northern and southern hemispheres. These areas are between latitudes 50 and 30 and the greatest concentration of wine growing is in Europe.

When and where the properties of fermented grape juice were first appreciated is a mystery. It is pleasing to think of some distant ancestor coming across an accidental example of wine and tasting it suspiciously, perhaps desperate to slake his thirst, gulping greedily and then realising a new sensation was being experienced, a unique sensation of pleasure, warmth and happiness. For that is what wine is: a physical essence of pleasure.

There is much evidence of wine drinking and the cultivation of vines in the earliest civilizations: in ancient Persia, in the land of the Pharaohs, in ancient Greece. There has been a word for wine in many languages: from Sanskrit *vena* to Greek *oinos*, Latin *vinum*, French *vin* and English *wine*.

One explanation of the discovery of wine concerns the Persian King Dsemsit, who was so fond of the grapes of his country that he had them stored in stone jars in cellars so they could be enjoyed out of season.

Left in this way, the grapes fermented and the people thought they had become poisonous. A rejected favourite of the king is said to have wanted to put an end to her unhappiness by drinking this poisonous liquid. She did so but returned to the court flushed and happy, so much so that she caught the eye of the king and was restored to his affections. It is the first known example of the power of wine to bring happiness.

According to the Greeks, wine was introduced by the god Bacchus or Dionysus; the god of pleasure, that other side of man, the complement of the rational self.

In the tales of Homer written about 1000 BC wine is part of the fabric of society described, and writers from Horace to Dante and Rabelais have expressed themselves on the subject of wine. For Dante it was 'bottled sunshine' and for the Psalmist it was simply 'Wine which maketh glad the heart of man'. Vines were cultivated and wine drunk in Egypt 3000 BC and the Egyptian god Osiris was 'The Lord of Wine and the Flood'. The intrepid Phoenicians carried on a thriving wine trade in 1500 BC through the Mediterranean and beyond, carrying their cargoes of wine to the farthest reaches of their trading routes.

Traditional wooden barrels *(above)* placed *bonde de côte* (with the bung on the side).

This 1877 vintage from Château La Mission Haut Brion *(left)* is one of the last pre-phylloxera years.

The château at Margaux and its gardens *(above)* have been extensively restored since 1974 when the estate was bought by André Mentzelopoulos.

This very old vine *(above)* is growing on the pebbly soil characteristic of the area. When an old vine is no longer productive, it will be uprooted and the soil allowed to rest for up to eight years.

The Bible has many references to wine, reflecting the significance of wine in the lives of the people of Israel; there was even a Talmudic law forbidding war at the time of the harvest.

Knowledge of wine spread from the Middle East to Greece, the great civilizing influence of the time and spread from there to Rome and the rest of Europe. The Greeks introduced wine into Europe sometime about 600 BC when they established the port of Massilia at what is now modern Marseilles. Greek colonies were founded on the Italian peninsula around 800 BC and a brisk wine trade was carried on. There was a pipeline at Sybaris to carry the wine from the cellars to the port.

Vines were grown and wine made in Ancient Rome, before the building of Rome. The Romans took to wine with abandon, as can be seen in the writings of the Romans from Virgil to Juvenal.

The vine is an indication of a settled way of life. It could not be cultivated by a migratory, wandering people but had to be tended by a people who had, as it were, put down roots.

Along with excellent roads and sound principles of administration, the industrious Romans spread the knowledge of wine throughout their world. The vine is as much a symbol of the conquest of Rome as the shield, as it was planted wherever Roman legions were stationed: in France, Germany and even England.

During the decline of the Roman Empire, the early church guarded the secrets of the cultivation of the vine. It is no accident

that wine, fundamental to life itself, became a part of the ritual of the church, the blood of Christ.

Monks planted vineyards wherever monasteries were established, to provide wine for their services and, as monks were also men, for themselves. It has been said that the fathers selected the best sites for their monasteries and the same can be said of their choice of vineyards, which were chosen with considerable skill. The many examples that survive could not be bettered for position, micro-climate and soil; the monks literally tasted the soil to see if it was pure.

The Clos de Vougeot in Burgundy are an example and nuns established vineyards in the Rheingau, introducing the noble *Riesling*. The churches of Europe have many architectural allusions to wine, reflecting the importance of wine in the life of the people.

Regulations governing the production of wine have been in operation for more than 2000 years and it has always been a favoured source of tax revenue.

The taste for wine grew in those countries which were producers and in those which were unable to produce it. The trade in wine begun by the Phoenicians continued, especially from France to the northern countries of Europe. Bordeaux was a great wine port, where wine from all parts of France was shipped to the countries of Belgium, Holland and England. It became part of England, as did the whole of Aquitaine, when Henry Plantagenet

Stainless steel fermentation tanks and German white oak casks and barrels *(left)* demonstrate the marriage of ancient and modern wine-making techniques.

This picture *(top)* shows the spirit of France with a bottle of Loudenne wine. Château Loudenne kept the black label until the early 1960s. This label for the 1895 Steinberg *(above)* is for the *Kabinett* variety.

The Ausone vineyard *(below)* is small and compact, so it is still economical to use a horse rather than a tractor to work the soil, which is regularly tilled especially in the growing season.

This colourful ceramic figure *(above)* is found in the Château La Mission Haut Brion *chais* where tastings take place. These vineyards at Pouilly-sur-Loire *(right)* are planted with Sauvignon. The soil is stony and chalky. Pouilly-sur-Loire is one of the villages which make wine for the Pouilly Blanc Fume *appellation*, made entirely from Sauvignon grapes.

became King of England. The busy port of Libourne on the Dordogne takes its name from Sir Roger de Leybourne, a knight who also gave his name to the Kent village of Leybourne. The cobbles in the steep streets of nearby St Emilion are said to have been used as ballast by English ships taking in cargoes of wine at Libourne.

The 18th century saw a dramatic and crucial development for the wine industry with the commercial use of glass bottles and cork stoppers. Bordeaux had a glassworks in 1723 and bottles were produced on a massive scale. The development of the bottle and cork led to the mystery of wine ageing and improving in the bottle, and also made it possible for people well beyond Europe to enjoy the wines; flourishing markets were soon opened up in the new world of North America.

The knowledge of vines and wine making spread from Europe throughout the world. It is now made in about 50 different countries, but Europe is still the centre of the wine industry.

During picking *(above)* the grapes are gathered by hand and put into baskets, which are then tipped into the *hotte* in which they are taken to the waiting trailer or lorry.

The only European countries where the vine is not cultivated are the Netherlands, Poland, Ireland, Denmark, Norway, Sweden and Finland. Europe produces about 80 per cent of the world's wine. There are major producers of wine in other parts of the world — the USSR and Argentina are examples — but they cannot be compared with Italy and France. In the league of producers, Italy comes first and is followed by France and Spain. The principal wine exporting countries follow the same pattern, with Italy in the lead, and the main wine importing countries are West Germany, the USSR, the United Kingdom and Switzerland.

Naturally enough, the wine producing countries of Europe show a marked taste for the wine they produce. Average per capita consumption in France, for example, is 95 litres a year; in Italy 93; in Portugal 70; Spain 64; followed by the United Kingdom and the United States which manage about 7 litres a year.

Europe's reputation as the heartland of the world's wine is based not on the volume of production but on the quality of the wine produced, as it provides more quality wine than any region on earth.

These bunches of Pinot Noir *(right)* have just been picked. The grapes are taken from the vineyard to the cellar where they are loaded into the destalker.

The miracle of wine has been recognized and appreciated in Europe for centuries, and the knowledge and love of wine is an expression of European civilization.

Indeed, appreciation of wine is evidence of the qualities that separate mankind from the rest of the animal kingdom. Intelligence, ingenuity, courage, the ability to love and communicate — all these qualities can be observed in many living creatures, but the appreciation of wine appears to be an exclusively human characteristic. It is concerned not only with satisfying a physical need but with something quite different. It belongs to that part of the mind from which poetry, music and art spring and, like them, it inspires the best and most generous impulses.

WINE MAKING

The quality of the soil *(above)* is a vital factor in the production of good wine. The monks who founded many of Europe's vineyards in the Middle Ages literally tasted the soil to see if it was pure.

Despite the centuries men have been making wine, despite the accumulated wisdom of generations of wine growers, despite the advances of science, wine remains mysterious.

Modern science has enabled chemists to analyse the constituents of wine — to identify the ethyl alcohol, acids, aldehydes, esters and minerals — but the knowledge gained, though valuable, does not answer all the questions.

We cannot say why one wine smells of raspberries and another of apples. The process of maturation contains many secrets, such as the way the final colour is achieved, the way one wine ages rapidly and another slowly, although they may share almost identical growing conditions.

Vines flourish in various conditions, from the green banks of the Rhine to the sun-soaked hills of the Rhône. It often grows on poor soil but the vine's roots go so deep that it can obtain the essential nutrients in what seem to be the most inhospitable of conditions.

The three factors that most influence the successful growing of vines are the grape variety, the climate and the soil. Experts differ about the order of priority, but these are the three principal points — not forgetting the element of human skill.

The generally accepted definition of wine is 'the fermented juice of freshly picked grapes', which is reasonable enough but not completely accurate. The grapes from which wine is made are not always freshly picked. In some cases they are left on the vine to wither so that a higher sugar content can be achieved.

Recioto, from the Valpolicella district, is made from grapes that have been dried in warehouses for some months. In Jerez they are dried in the sun to increase the sugar content.

Grapes left on the vine to dry produce some of the world's most noble wines — the *Sauternes* of France, the *Tokay* of Hungary and the *Trockenbeerenauslese* of Germany.

For wine growers the weather is of critical importance, as it is to all farmers. In some European countries it is more unpredictable than others: the wine grower in Moselle, for example, will have different worries than the wine grower in the Medoc, but both will have problems.

What the wine grower hopes for is a judicious blend of sun and rain at appropriate times in the cycle of growth. A mild spring should be followed by a sunny June; sun with a little rain in August; a fine September with the occasional shower and a dry, sunny October. June is the month for blossom and pollination (which governs the quantity of grapes that will be grown). Heavy rain in June can be a disaster as the rain washes the pollen from the blossom. Frost and hail are the two greatest threats. Frost can devastate the young vine shoots in the spring, and hail in August can tear the leaves to shreds.

It takes 100 days to produce ripe grapes from flowering. Even if there are no disasters there will be minor changes — a little more or less rain or sunshine at certain times which will play its part in

The type and age of the vine *(above)* are also of paramount importance..

Human knowledge and experience is a major factor in the production of good wine. Here *(left)* the long-standing *maître de chais* at Mouton Rothschild (Raoul Blondin) checks the colour of the wine during its first year.

After picking, the grapes are put into a trailer and then taken to the winery *(above)*.

Care of the vineyards is of prime importance at all times. This includes tilling the soil between the rows of vines *(above)*.

the final harvest. Each year is different from another and so is the wine produced.

The culmination of the year comes in September and October with the harvesting of the grapes. Vast armies of men and women gather throughout Europe to pick the grapes which will be made into wine; cheap, cheerful *vin de pays* or aristocratic and exclusive wine for the collector.

Fermentation turns the grape juice into wine. When collected, the grapes are put into vats and the skins of the grapes broken. The way this is done varies from country to country. Traditionally it was done by treading the grapes with bare feet, which still happens in a few areas. It might be done lightly or hardly at all, or it might be done with large presses, as is the case in most commercial operations of any size.

The object of breaking the skin is to allow the yeast cells which form on the skin to contact the sugar in the grape and turn it into alcohol. This is the heart of the wine process, a demonstration of the idea that wine is bottled sunshine. The grapes contain sugar which is formed by the sun and which turns into alcohol during fermentation.

During fermentation the cap of skins is mixed with the fermenting must — often with poles *(right)*.

Barrels are thoroughly cleaned before the new wine is put into them *(above)*. Modern technology has dramatically speeded up the bottling process *(left)*.

The action of fermentation starts quickly and continues vigorously, with ever-increasing bubbles appearing in the grape juice. Carbon dioxide is also formed as the sugar is converted into alcohol.

Yeast cells cannot survive in more than 15 per cent alcohol so in some cases, where the grapes have a very high sugar content, the yeast cells cease to function before the sugar is converted into alcohol. However, the sugar content *is* usually converted before the 15 per cent alcohol level is reached.

After pressing and fermentation, the wine is drawn off into containers. In ordinary commercial wine, it is fed into large vats and left until fermentation stops. The impurities are filtered off and the wine is ready for bottling quite quickly.

Wines of quality are treated with much more care. They spend at least two years in the barrel, during which time the wine is transferred to new clean barrels so that the impurities and deposits are gradually separated.

After two years, the wine is put into bottles and it is during this stage that the great wines become great. Over the years they develop their individual character, bouquet, colour and flavour.

Lafite has one of the largest collections of old wines in France *(left)*. The bottles are carefully recorked at intervals. These examples come from pre-phylloxera years.

The length of the maturing process varies greatly. Some wines reach a peak after four or five years, some after 10 or 20 years. There have been many examples of wine which is perfectly drinkable after more than 100 years. The explanation for the longevity of the wine lies in the kind of grape from which the wine is made. Some, such as the *Cabernet Sauvignon*, are renowned for the longevity of the wines they produce.

Wine is a living thing, like a man or a tree. It changes, grows, develops and with care and love and luck matures from fiery youth to benign age. This transformation takes place in the bottle, a transformation that would not have been possible before the introduction of the cork.

The cork provides the element of oxygen which allows the wine to develop in the bottle. Air reaches the wine through the tiny holes in the cork itself and through the space between the cork and the neck of the bottle. It is important, when storing wine, to make sure the bottle is on its side so that the cork and wine meet. If the cork is left to dry it becomes useless. Generally red wines mature more than white wines. Red wines are made from black grapes and the colour comes from the skin during fermentation.

White wines are made from white grapes, although black grapes can be used. They are usually ready to drink much earlier than red wines, but the great white wines — such as *Château d'Yquem* and *Montrachet* — will grow and develop over many years.

There is an extraordinary variety of white wines. Even the term white wine is misleading as the colour of white wine can vary from the deepest gold to delicate green or flowery yellow. The character of white wines varies from the honeyed fulness of a *Monbazillac* to the spring freshness of a flowery-scented *Moselle*.

When white wine is made, the grapes are separated from the skins quickly and the grapes are pressed as soon as they come into the winery. Fermentation is exactly the same as for red wine. Once the fermentation is complete, the wine is transferred to vats or, in the case of quality wines, to clean barrels. Temperature is critical to the fermentation process — if it is too cold, the yeast cells will not work properly; if it is too hot, the fermentation may be too violent, leading to unbalanced wine.

The critical time in the making of white wine is the spring when an increase in temperature may cause a second fermentation. Once this period is past, the wine is bottled and ready for further maturation in the bottle or for drinking, in the case of ordinary *vin de table*.

The delicate pink of rosé comes from black grapes from which rosé wine is usually made. The colour comes from brief contact with skins; not more than 24 hours. During this time sufficient colour is absorbed to give the distinctive pink and, as there has been no absorption of tannin, the wine is light in character and

These wooden presses *(below)* are in use, their lids are not fully down. This type of press is best suited to red grapes, which are more robust than white, because the tannin and colour which this type of press extracts are more necessary in red wine. A horizontal press which allows greater control over the pressing is better for white grapes, which need more delicate treatment.

Cleanliness is crucial in wine-making. These barrels *(below)* are being soaked, both to clean them and to make sure they are watertight.

A horizontal press *(below)* suitable
for white grapes.

These Semillion grapes *(above)* have noble rot. The characteristic discolouring and shrivelling can be seen, as well as the fungus-like growth.

much more like a white wine than a red wine. As with white wines, rosé is bottled young and drunk young.

Sweet wines are a contradiction in a sense as the natural process of fermentation is to make dry wines. The yeast cells work on the sugar content, turning it into alcohol and only complete their work when all the sugar has been converted or the alcohol content has risen to a high level of 15 per cent.

Some grapes have such a high concentration of sugar that the yeast cells are unable to convert all the sugar before the 15 per cent level of alcohol has been reached. The wine from these grapes is sweet and has a high alcohol content. Examples are *Sauternes* where the grape is picked late and the sugar content is increased by a fungal condition called 'noble rot'. Another example is the expensive *Trockenbeerenauslese* from Germany. These are superb wines, produced naturally from some of the finest grapes in the world.

Where the natural sugar content of the grape is not high enough to produce the required level of sweetness, the winemaker lends a hand by introducing alcohol to interrupt the fermentation

The slatey soil of the Mosel region *(left)* gives the best wine a characteristic flavour; a quite extraordinary delicacy and vivacity.

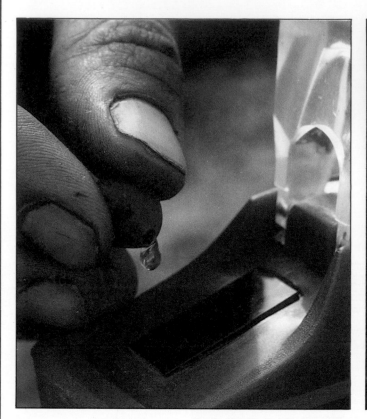

Sugar levels are checked at many stages in the wine's development. A refractometer *(above)* can be used in the vineyard or in the cellar.

Taking a sample of a very young wine from an oak *foudre* with a pipette *(above)*.

process. In this way the 15 per cent level of alcohol is reached before the sugar has been converted, interrupting the action of yeast cells and leaving the required level of sweetness.

Other methods of intervening in the fermentation process before the sugar has been converted are refrigeration (to prevent the action of the yeast cells) and pasteurization (which kills the yeast cells). These methods would never be applied to quality wines which are the result of natural processes. Intervention of this kind is for cheap, popular wines.

Fortified wines such as port, sherry and Madeira are examples of the addition of alcohol to wine. With sherry, alcohol is added after fermentation to give dry sherry its highly valued dry flavour. If sweet sherry is required, sweet wine is added.

In the making of port, alcohol is added during fermentation which has the effect of killing off the yeast cells and gives a wine of high alcohol and sweetness. Port developed from the need to quench the British thirst for wine during one of the many disagreements with France — this time at the beginning of the 18th century — when war interefered in the wine trade between the two countries.

Sparkling wines, as befits their character, have become associated with joyful, festive occasions. The most famous type of sparkling wine is *champagne*, which is named from the region where it is made and is the only sparkling wine in the world permitted to carry the name, although wines are made in a similar way in other countries.

The *champagne* method is the natural one, as in all good wines, and involves a secondary fermentation in the bottle. After the first fermentation before bottling, a second fermentation takes place in the bottle. This is much less vigorous than the first one and produces carbon dioxide. It is this gas that escapes when the wine is uncorked, producing that welcome, celebratory stream of foaming wine and that deliciously lively wine.

The *méthode champenoise* is used to make other sparkling wines — the sparkling wine of Saumur from the Loire is an excellent example. This method is costly as it requires a considerable amount of time and manpower, but there are cheaper methods.

The simplest is to pump carbon dioxide into the wine, as is done in the production of simple sparkling wines from Germany. Another method for cheaper wines is to include a second fermentation by adding sugar and yeast to a sealed tank.

The grape or grape varieties used in the making of a wine is the key element in its eventual character, just as the parents are the principal element in the formation of the child. Yet different grape varieties planted in different regions can produce widely different results. A grape planted in France may produce wine of the most distinguished kind, while the same grape variety grown in another country with an apparently similar environment and climate may produce wine of only modest quality.

An essential part of the winegrower's skill is in selecting the right grape variety for his particular area. The micro-climate — the immediate locality of a vineyard — can produce surprising differences. In Bordeaux there is often a marked difference between wine made from identical grapes grown on adjoining properties. In some wine growing areas a single grape variety is used; in others a variety of grapes.

Cabernet Sauvignon is the great grape of the Médoc — and it has been highly successful throughout the world — but in Bordeaux a number of varieties are used in the making of the famous red wine. *Cabernet Sauvignon* gives the wine its hardness and is strong in tannin which gives the wine the ability to age well.

Cabernet Franc is also used. It has a softer, fruitier character than *Cabernet Sauvignon* and is widely used in the red wines of the Loire, especially in the red wines of Chinon and Bourgueil — neighbouring areas producing light, elegant red wines which are said to be recognizable by the bouquet, the *Bourgueil* smelling of raspberries and the *Chinon* of violets.

Merlot is the most important grape in the best wines of St Emilion and Pomerol. It provides wine of high alcohol content and good colour and is also used in the making of Bergerac wines and the 'black' wines of Cahors.

Single grape varieties are used in the making of the famous wines of Burgundy. *Pinot Noir* is the grape from which the

The bubbles in the fermentation vat for red grapes *(above)* show the carbon dioxide produced during fermentation.

Cabernet Sauvignon   Pinot Noir   Merlot

Picking grapes by hand *(right, far right)* is an integral part of the wine-making process.

Sangiovese

Riesling

Silvaner

Chardonnay

splendid wines of the region are made.

Gamay is the grape of *Beaujolais*. The scented, fruity wine which is produced in Beaujolais can be drunk young and simple or as a wine of considerable distinction from one of the nine major districts such as Fleurie or Moulin-à-Vent. In recent years, young *Beaujolais* has become highly popular as *Beaujolais Nouveau*, which is pressed quickly and released for consumption on the first possible date, November 15.

Syrah is one of the major grape varieties of wines from the Northern Rhône area. Said to be introduced from Syria, it produces big wines of great longevity.

Grenache is widely used in red wines of the Southern Rhône and produces wine of deep colour and high alcohol.

Carignana is a strongly perfumed grape widely grown in Provence and Languedoc-Roussillon.

Sangiovese is one of the most widely grown grapes in Italy and is one of the major influences on *Chianti* and produces *Brunello*.

Nebbiolo is used in the making of *Barolo*, the favourite wine of Julius Caesar, and is a classic variety of Piedmont.

Dolcetto is a popular grape variety, producing highly flavoured red wine of strong taste.

Barbera is an Italian grape which can produce wines of high quality and alcohol content, given time.

Chardonnay is one of the great white grape varieties of France; the grape from which white Burgundy is made, including the rich, elegant and dry *Montrachet*.

Sauvignon is widely planted in the Western side of France, from the Loire to the Dordogne, and is used in the making of a range of white wines such as *Entre-Deux-Mers* and *Haut-Poitou* and the distinctive wines of Sancère and Pouilly Blanc Fume.

Semillon is used with *Sauvignon* to produce the great sweet wines of Sauternes and the great dry wines of Graves.

Chenin Blac or *Pineau de Loire* is used for dry, demi-sec and sweet white wines. Widely used in the Loire, it produces some remarkable fine wines — for example, *Vouvray*, which Rabelais described as 'silken wine'.

Muscadet is the name of the grape from which the unique wine is made in the Nantes region at the Atlantic side of the Loire. Dry, refreshing, it seems to carry an echo of the sea, a tang of the Atlantic. Bliss with fish, especially with shellfish.

Trebbiano is one of the most popular white grape varieties in Italy and produces a variety of wine in different regions.

The *Riesling* grape is the glory of German wine and produces the great wines of the Moselle and Rhine. It is notable for its bouquet, full and flowery, and can produce wine of the highest quality.

Gewurztraminer is highly successful in Alsace and Germany and is also known for its aromatic qualities.

Sylvaner is a variety used in many parts of Germany and Alsace producing light, delicate wines with a pleasing bouquet.

The Merlot vine *(below)* is the
second red grape variety
of Bordeaux.

QUALITY CONTROL

Tasting a white must from a stainless steel fermentation vat *(above)*.

Faced with the scale, range and variety of European wines, the inexperienced wine drinker is likely to falter when attempting to choose a bottle of wine to accompany the family meal. However, there is a considerable amount of detailed information on bottle labels which can help guide the uncertain hand to the right choice for the right occasion.

Regulations of the European Economic Community require wine-producing member countries to provide certain information on their bottles. The compulsory information includes country of origin; the amount of wine in the bottle; the name and address of the bottler responsible; the name of the specified region of origin — in the case of quality wine — or the term 'table wine' for basic wine.

Optional information can be included such as the type of wine (red, white, rosé); alcoholic strength; sweet or dry; the name and address of the shipper or retailer and awards which the wine has been given. Wines from outside the EEC must observe the same compulsory information as EEC wines and the name and address of the importer if they are bottled outside the EEC. Wines from non-member countries are known only as *vin*, wine, etc.

Table wine (*vin de table*, *vina tavola*, *Tafelwein*, etc) is light wine produced in and from grapes in EEC member countries. These wines usually come from one country, but where they are made from a blend of wines from different EEC countries, the label must show where the wines come from.

These table wines cannot carry any further description of quality or precise geographical origin but there is another category of table wine called 'table wine with geographical origin'. These wines can show more than the country of origin and can say where they originate from in their country. In place of the words 'table wine', they can be described as *vin de pays* in France, *Landwein* in Germany or *vino tipico* in Italy. This description can accompany the name of the geographical area — for example, *Vin de Pays de l'Aude*.

As in much else concerning wine, France has been a pioneer in the search for controlling the quality and authenticity of wines. The French *Appellation d'Origine Contrôlée* was introduced in France in the 1930s in an attempt to cope with the confusion in France after the First World War when wine was incorrectly and fraudulently labelled.

The letters AC or AOC, *Appellation Controlée* and *Appellation d'Origine Controlée*, are not, however, a guarantee of quality. They are a guarantee of authenticity and ensure that the wine comes from where it is said to come from. The name of a particular region can be included; *Appellation Saumur Controlée*, for example.

The *Appellation Controlée* regulations affect quality though, as they govern almost every aspect of the wine: grape variety, alcohol level, methods of pruning, yield per hectare.

Below the level of AC wines are VDQS, *Vine de Limite de*

When bottling, a vacuum is created in the headspace above the bottled wine before the cork is inserted *(above)*.

Tasting the wine before *écoulage* *(left)*.

Examining the purity of the wine in the cellars at Bodrogszeg, Hungary *(left)*.

Acidity levels are carefully monitored throughout the fermentation process *(right)*. Wine with too low an acidity can be rather fragile.

Qualité Supérieure, which is designed to encourage good local wine from specific regions. These are generally better than simple table wines and some are particularly good value — *Corbière*, for example. Some experts say that some VDQS wines can be superior to some AC wines because the VDQS system is stricter in some ways. In general, VDQS wines are cheaper than AC wines.

So the buyer of French wine has a simple guide to quality from *vin de table*, *vin de pays*, VDQS and AOC.

Germany has the most strictly controlled wine laws and German wine labels provide the most precise information of any European country. The highest level of quality is the *Qualitätswein mit Prädikat* (QmP). Wines permitted to carry this description never have sugar added.

As a wine-producing country, Germany has the disadvantage of being on a northerly latitude, although its uncertain summers are responsible for the unique character of the best German wine. As sunshine is relatively low, certainly when compared with the great wine-abundant areas of the southern half of France, it is the practice to add sugar to wine, when the natural sugar content is low, except in the case of QmP wines.

QmP wines also carry additional information on quality or ripeness; starting with *Kabinett* and rising through *Spätlese*, *Auslese*, *Beerenauslese* and culminating in the splendour of *Trockenbeerenauslese*. The second classification of quality is *Qualitätswein* (QbA). Wines displaying this term are wines of quality to which sugar has been added during the making of the wine. QmP and QbA wines carry a quality testing number after they have been tested for vintage, analysis and taste.

Below these two categories is *Landwein*, which is similar to the

French *vin de pays* and indicates the wine is from a specific region. *Tafelwein* is simply table wine which is basic wine without any special claims to distinction.

The way in which German wine is classified is fundamentally different from the system followed in France. In Germany, the sugar content is the critical factor when assessing quality. The greatest wine a grower can produce is a *Trockenbeerenauslese*, which is wine with the greatest natural sugar content.

The location of the vineyard does not have anything like the same importance as in France where the classification system is based on the origin of the wine and where the name of the vineyard is a guarantee of quality — for example, *Château Ausone* or *Moulin-à-Vent*.

Although the origin of the wine does not have the official importance as in France it does matter, of course, as individual areas and growers are known for certain kinds of wines. Generally the more detailed the information the better quality the wine is likely to be. Germany is divided into a number of wine regions, the best known of which are Mosel-Saar-Ruwer, Rheingau,

Chianti is one of the best known
Italian wines permitted to carry the
DOC classification *(right)*.

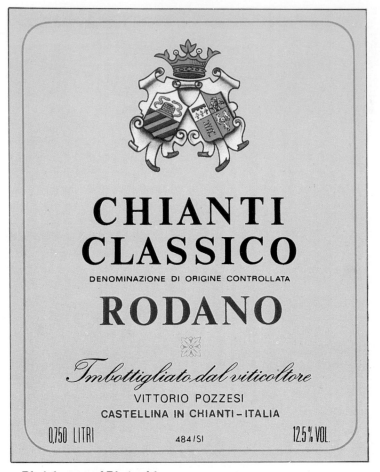

Rheinhesse and Rheinpfalz.

Traditionally, Italy had a rather relaxed attitude towards wine laws. It is a country of wine and the general feeling was that it was there to be enjoyed.

However, in recent times there has been a considerable effort to provide tighter control of wine produced. In 1963 the Italian government introduced new categories for quality wines. The basic classification is the DOC or *Denominazione di Origine Controllata*. This is similar to the French *Appellation Controlée*. Essentially, DOC wines are subject to regulations governing grape varieties used, the areas of production, minimum alcohol content, and period of ageing.

Valpolicella, *Chianti* and *Asti Spumante* are some of the best known wines carrying the DOC classification, but there are more than 200 wines permitted to carry the classification.

The highest classification of quality for Italian wine is the DOCG — *Denominazione di Origine Controllata e Garantita*. The regulations governing this classification are similar to those of the DOC but they cover the size of the bottle in which the wine is sold and each bottle carries a seal of guarantee. The classification is quite rare, few wines are permitted to carry this distinction and they include *Barolo* and *Barbaresco* from

Piedmont and *Brunello di Montalcino* and *Vino Nobile de Montepulciano* from Tuscany.

Spain is another country where wine laws have been strengthened with a consequent improvement of the wines grown and an enhanced reputation abroad.

The *Denominación de Origen* governs the production of wine in defined areas and is similar to the French *Appellation Controlée*.

Wine from Portugal's eight official wine regions, *Regio Demarcada*, have a *Selo de Garantia* on the bottle which shows the wine has passed official quality control tests.

Wine labels *(above)* contain information regarding the quality and origin of the wine.

FRANCE

Robert Ampeau *(above)*, owner of Domaine Ampeau, tastes a wine in his cellar. Behind him are wines ageing in Burgundian *pièces* and maturing in the bottle.

In the world of wine, France is more than a mere country. It is a continent in which all kinds of wine, particularly of quality wine, can be found: from the astringency of *Muscadet* to the elegance of *Bordeaux*; the nobility of *Burgundy* to the power of the *Rhône*.

France's tradition of wine growing is a statement about the nature of the country. Other countries share France's concern for painting and literature but the love of wine expresses the difference between France and others, it illustrates a certain civilized approach to the business of living.

Wine is grown in almost every part of France, from Alsace to the Pyrenees. The main wine growing areas are Bordeaux, Burgundy, Loire, Rhône, Champagne, Alsace, Languedoc-Roussillon and Provence, and Jura.

Bordeaux is the first of the wine-growing regions, an area varied and rich in wine, a country in itself. It is a place where one could stay for ever without ever exploring further, as John Donne remarked in another context.

It is the land of the châteaux; an estimated 10,000 châteaux produce wine. A château in Bordeaux need not mean a fairy-tale castle — although some are — but can equally well be applied to a small estate with an ordinary house.

About 200 châteaux produce the great wines for which Bordeaux is known throughout the world. These are the princes of the royal blood such as: Château Margaux; Château Haut-Brion, Château Ausone, Château Lafite. Unfortunately, most of us are as likely to become intimately acquainted with them as we are with princes. Their exclusivity means they are very expensive and for most of us they remain objects of veneration but no more than that.

Thankfully, Bordeaux produces much quality wine at prices which the ordinary wine buyer can afford. It is the largest producer of fine wine in the world, both red and white.

The city and port of Bordeaux is at the centre of the wine trade. It has been a port for more than a thousand years. In fact, it is not on the sea but some 100 kilometres from the Atlantic, on the banks of the Garonne. Its access to the sea is via the Gironde, which is formed where the Garonne and Dordogne rivers converge.

Bordeaux is a handsome city with a patrician quality entirely appropriate to the centre of the kingdom of wine. Nowadays, wine is no longer the principal element of the business of the port and evidence of modern industry can be seen around the city in factories housing automobile and engineering industry, but Bordeaux remains, for most people, essentially a centre of wine.

Claret is the word the English use for red *Bordeaux*; the word comes from an old French word describing wine made of red and white grapes but the term is now used only for red wine. England has had a long and close association with Bordeaux since the 12th century and was a part of England when Henry Plantagenet became King of England in 1154. It remained so throughout the

These oak storage barrels *(above)* are 228 litre Burgundy *pièces*.

The Hermitage vineyards in the northern Rhône are dominated by the very steep granite slopes of the Massif Central which rise up from the river *(left)*. The Syrah grape variety flourishes here in some of the oldest vineyards in France.

These containers, called *hottes (right)*, are carried on the backs of pickers who walk up and down the rows of vines collecting the grapes gathered into baskets by other pickers. The contents of the *hottes* are then put into a trailer or cart and taken to the *chais*.

An aristocratic home for a wine of great breeding — Château Palmer, producer of one of Bordeaux's finest wines *(below)*.

The château and gardens at Ducru-Beaucaillou *(above)* are among the most carefully maintained in the whole of the Bordeaux vineyard area. The long, low architectural style is typical of the Gironde.

At Château Palmer, large red painted oak fermentation vats *(above)* are used. There are 14 vats in all. This traditional practice is felt to aid the quality of the wine.

Hundred Years' War until it was restored to France.

The association between Bordeaux and England was so fruitful for trade that the people of Bordeaux wanted to remain a part of England and took the side of the English during the conflict.

The decline in trade between Bordeaux and England that followed the return of Bordeaux to France was restored by the growing importance of Holland as a major customer — a country, like England, which showed a passion for a product it was unable to produce.

The 18th century was a high point for the wine industry. The development of blown glass bottles and corks marked a new development in the expansion of wine exports as the wine could be conserved more efficiently. From this point, exports to the farthest corners of the commercial world became possible, particularly to North America.

The Napoleonic wars interfered with the wine trade between England and Bordeaux once again when trade was suspended. England found an opportunity to do its duty by its favourite region a little later when Gladstone lowered the duty on imported wines in 1860, an act that led to a boom in the imports of wine from France, especially from Bordeaux. Englishmen have been praying for a leader as enlightened as Gladstone ever since.

The wine districts of Bordeaux are grouped around the city: Côte de Blaye; Côte de Bourg; Fronsac; Pomerol; St Emilion; Côte de Bordeaux; Entre-Deux-Mers; Sauternes; Graves and Médoc. The system of classification of wines is precise but is also complicated. A difficulty is that there are a number of ways of assessing the quality wines, some of which overlap. Basically, the classification of quality, in ascending order, is *Bordeaux*; *Bordeaux Supérieure*; a wine district such as Entre-Deux-Mers; a commune name such as St Estèphe. Each of these wines, although different in quality, would be entitled to carry the *Appellation d'Origine Controlée* and most would carry the name of the château.

Wines carrying a district name — for example, Graves — may

Drainage channels *(above)*, both natural streams called *jalles* and man-made canals, help drain the vineyards. This is a typical procedure in the Médoc. In the steepest part of the Lafite vineyards *(above right)*, the large pebbles characteristic of the soil in the Médoc can be seen.

be from a single vineyard or a blend of wines of the district. A wine with a basic *Bordeaux* appellation may also be from a specific vineyard or it can be a blend of Bordeaux wines. In the St Emilion area, villages which are not allowed to carry the famous name itself are allowed to use their own name in association with that of St Emilion, thus enjoying a certain reflected glory.

Above these categories of quality, and running parallel to them, is the system of classification of the leading wines of Bordeaux. It can appear a somewhat clumsy method but, while there are reasons for criticism, is generally accepted as a system that has demonstrated that it works.

The system was introduced at the instigation of Louis Napoleon III for the great Paris International Exhibition of 1855. Louis Napoleon was determined that there should be some order in the way the great wines of Bordeaux were to be judged and so the *Classement des Grands Crus de la Gironde* was introduced. The wine merchants of Bordeaux were given the task of assessing the wines of their region in terms of quality. The yardstick they used was the price the wines had commanded over several years for then, as now, the best wines are the most expensive.

The most expensive wines were listed and divided into five categories — *crus* or growths. Some 60 wines were included in this Burke's Peerage of wine; a collection of the most exclusive names in the world of wines. As in all such judgements, especially in Bordeaux where the deep sense of pride of the wine growers was involved, there were protests about the final list. It is true that anomalies existed. Some great wines were not included; *Pomerol* and *St Emilion* were completely ignored. The reasons for these omissions are complicated. The distinguished wine writer and grower, Alexis Lichine, has suggested that snobbery was one of the causes as, at the time the list was being drawn up, St Emilion was something of a backwater in Bordeaux wine circles. Whatever the reasons, the cries of indignation reverberate to

The practice of making barrels *(above)* used to be more common, but expense has made it impractical for most châteaux.

this day.

At the top of the listing are four *premiers crus* — *Château Lafite-Rothschild*; *Château Latour*, *Château Margaux* and *Château Haut-Brion*. Below these are other great wines in groups of from second to fifth growths. The numerical listing causes problems because it suggests a difference of quality which may not exist. A fifth-growth (*cinquième cru*) may be superior to a third-growth (*troisième cru*).

When *St Emilion* and *Pomerol* were given their own system of classification, the numerical system was largely ignored. *St Emilion*, for example, was divided into *premier grand cru* classes and *grand cru* classes.

Below the classification of these great wines is a much larger group of Bourgeois growths which is sub-divided into *cru exceptionel*, *cru bourgeois supérieur* and *cru bourgeois*. Wines in this group are sometimes the equal of those in the classification of great wines of the region and many represent excellent value.

The task of identifying the best wines of the region is further complicated by the fact that the thousands of owners of châteaux

The first pruning after the vintage takes place in November. In the Mersault-Perrières vineyard *(above)* the vines are being cut back and the wood burnt. The larger branches are taken outside the vineyard and burnt, while the smaller ones are burnt in iron braziers in the vineyard.

in Bordeaux believe they are producing the region's finest wine. This pride in the individual château is reflected in the prominence given on the labels of Bordeaux wines to the place where the wine originated.

RED WINES OF BORDEAUX

Médoc provides the classic claret which is seen at its highest level in wines from the communes of St Estèphe, Pauillac, St Julien and Margaux. From the gravelly soil of this peninsula more than 50 million bottles of wine a year are produced.

The Médoc has two appellations — Haut Médoc and Médoc. The first includes all the finest wines of the area while the latter produces wines which are excellent but not as inspired as those of the Haut Médoc.

The wines of Pauillac include three of the four premier growths. *Pauillac* can be long-lived; big, elegant with a powerful bouquet.

St Julien wines are a touch lighter but with great finesse. *Margaux* is more delicate, perfumed, subtle. *St Estèphe* has a characteristic fruitiness and the commune produces many excellent bourgeois growths.

The Médoc produces more quality red wine than anywhere in the world and is fascinating because of the many variations in the wine produced. St Emilion is perhaps the most famous name of Bordeaux and is certainly one of the prettiest towns in the region with its steep cobbled streets — the stones used are said to have been brought in by English ships as ballast when they were shipping wine from Libourne in the 18th century.

The wines of St Emilion are more powerful than those of the Médoc and have a higher level of alcohol. Yet they are ready to be drunk, often from three or four years.

The district is in two parts. The first is the area around the town itself and wines from this area carry the appellation *St Emilion*. The second part is the group of six communes which are entitled to use the proud name of *St Emilion* with their own — for example, *Lussac St Emilion* and *Sables St Emilion*.

The best wine comes from the hills around the town, the Côtes St Emilion. Here are the famous names of the district — Château Ausone, Clos Foutet, Pavie and so on.

Rather confusingly, the area below the town is called Graves St Emilion, but it has nothing to do with the Graves district south of Bordeaux. The word refers to the gravel in the soil which appears to have a beneficial effect on the vines. It adjoins Pomerol and produces superb, velvety wines such as *Château Cheval Blanc* and *Figeac* among many others.

Pomerol, like *St Emilion*, matures early and can be drunk from three or four years, although the great *Pomerol* vintages will last many years, as long as just about any red wine.

This colourful ceramic figure *(right)* is in the *chais* of Château La Mission Haut Brion, where tastings take place.

Château La Mission Haut Brion *(left)*. At the near end can be seen the chapel built by the Lazarite order. The order lost control of the estate during the French Revolution.

The smallest of the red wine districts of Bordeaux, Pomerol produces a considerable amount of red wine and its greatest name is *Château Pétrus*, a wine ranking with the finest growths of the Médoc. Indeed, the wines of Pomerol bear a resemblance to those of the Médoc and are lighter than St Emilion wines. They are beautiful in colour, powerful and gentle and the wine is notable for its bouquet which is said to carry a hint of truffles, the treasure of the Périgord.

North of Pomerol is Lalande de Pomerol where the wines are not as great as Pomerol itself but which has some notable growths such as *Siaurac* and *Teysson*.

Graves is generally regarded as the home of Bordeaux's dry white wines but it also produces a large amount of red wine, perhaps a quarter of its total production. Proof of its ability to produce the finest red wine is *Château Haut Brion*, a first growth Bordeaux, one of the top four red wines in the 1855 classification of the leading wines of Bordeaux. There are other great growers of red wines in Graves — for example, Château La Mission and Château Pape-Clément whose vines were first planted in the 14th century by the Bishop of Bordeaux who later became Pope. Graves red wine, it is widely agreed, has a unique character — powerful, elegant and individual.

Less expensive red wines come from the Côtes de Bourg, the centre of which is the ancient town of Bourg. These red wines often represent good value and have a certain similarity to those of St Emilion, the most Burgundian of Bordeaux wines.

Blaye produces more white than reds but the reds are probably better than the white. They tend to be lighter than those of Bourg and mature earlier.

Fronsac is one of the prettiest parts of the Bordeaux region with lovely views over the fair, green hills of the Dordogne. The wines have great character and should not be drunk too young. They have a similarity to the full red wine of St Emilion and those of the Côtes de Fronsac have a distinct spiciness.

The red wines of Côtes de Bordeaux are inexpensive but good. This appellation is an indication of wines which are well balanced, agreeable, good in themselves and without the pretension of some wines of Bordeaux.

WHITE WINES OF BORDEAUX

Bordeaux produces at least as much white wine as it does red and the diversity of the wine produced is as remarkable.

Graves, while it produces red wines of great quality, is better known for its white wines. The name *Graves* is a general term for white wine. Simple *Graves* is white wine which contains 10 per cent of alcohol; it becomes *Graves Supérieur* when it achieves 12 per cent alcohol.

Characteristically, *Graves* is dry but with an interestingly full flavour. Unusually, châteaux which produce good red wine will also produce good white wine; even the great *Haut Brion* has a white wine which is said to be very good.

Entre-Deux-Mers lies between the Garonne and Dordogne. It's a vast area producing, as befits its name (between two seas), white wines of the middle range, between sweet and dry, which are enormously popular. The drier wines of the region, and those of Graves, go well with the fat oysters from the nearby bay of Arcachon. Bordeaux also produces some of the finest sweet (known as *liquorex*) white wines in France.

The glory of this type of wine is *Sauternes*, the wine from the golden *Sauvignon* and *Sémillon* grapes which are left unpicked on the vine until October, full of sugar and subject to the condition known as 'noble rot', a fungus which develops when the grape is over-ripe.

These grapes produce wine which is sweet but high in alcohol. Describing the wines of Sauternes has stretched the vocabulary of many poets — 'nectar of the gods' and 'exaggeration of the exquisite' are some of the more prosaic terms used.

The best, and most expensive, wine of Sauternes is *Château d'Yquem*. While this wine may be too expensive for most there are many other good *Sauternes* which demonstrate the extraordinary character of this wine — sweet but never cloying, full and complex, golden as the sun.

The wines of Sauternes may be drunk young, after three years or so, but the best should be left for 10 years and, for those with

The medieval Château d'Yquem *(top)* has been kept in good condition. Concerts are held in the picturesque central courtyard. Yquem's *maître de chais* is Guy Latrille *(above)*. He has taken some wine from the cask with a pipette and is spitting it out after tasting. The vineyards of Yquem *(left)*.

Sauternes vineyards in a morning mist *(right)*.

patience and a firm belief in their own longevity, they can mature for a century.

Barsac adjoins the Sauternes district and can be described as Barsac or under the Sauternes appellation. The sweet white wines of this commune share many characteristics of the wines of Sauternes — colour, power, sweetness — but are less rich.

Sweet white wines come from the areas around Sauternes, from Cerons and Graves, for example. The Cerons appellation covers three communes: Cerons, Illats and Podensac. The sweet white wine of Cerons resembles *Sauternes* but is rather lighter and has a personal style. Excellent sweet white wines are produced in the southern part of the Graves district and are labelled as *Graves Supérieur*. Other excellent sweet white wines come from Cadillac, Sainte-Croix-du-Mont and Luopiac.

BURGUNDY

The wines of Burgundy have come to be associated with qualities such as joviality, fulness and nobility just as wines of the Loire are associated with freshness and those of the Médoc with elegance.

Like all generalizations, it is not completely accurate and can be completely misleading. The variety of red and white wines produced in Burgundy ranges from big and powerful to delicate and subtle.

The name of Burgundy is an English corruption of the French word for the region, 'Bourgogne'. It is not a single entity like Bordeaux but a number of widely separated areas — like a string of islands running from Chablis in the north to the southern tip of Beaujolais about 22 miles away.

In the six defined areas of Burgundy — Chablis, Côte d'Or (comprising Côtes de Nuits and Côtes de Beaune), Côte Chalonnaise, Maconnais and Beaujolais — an almost bewildering variety of wine is produced, from wines of aristocratic pedigree and vast prices to simple country wines which anyone can afford.

Burgundy was part of the ancient Duchy of Burgundy. At the heart of France, it has been at the centre of the country's history.

The monastic orders, especially the Benedictines and Cistercians, played an important part in the development of vines and viticulture. Many orders were given gifts of vineyards which were tended to produce wine for use in the ritual of the Christian church. The vineyards of these old monastic estates survive today in many parts of Burgundy such as Clos de Vougeot. The siting of these vineyards, carried out by people without any knowledge of biochemistry and the consituents of soil in the early Middle Ages, could not be improved upon today.

The French Revolution put an end to large estates held by the Church. The large and wealthy holdings were confiscated and distributed among small farmers who often divided them still

The great Clos St Jacques *(left)*.

further. The result is that Burgundy is a region of small wine growers and of vineyards which often have a number of owners.

Wine from the same vineyard in the same year can be quite different depending on the skill of the grower, the age of the vines and other factors such as where the vines are grown in the *climat*, as the vineyards are known in Burgundy.

The Burgundian equivalent of *château* is *domaine,* but these are unlike the châteaux of Bordeaux which are often single units under one owner. In Burgundy the wine of the domaine may come from separate grapes grown in separate vineyards and sold under a separate name but made in the same cellar.

Burgundy does not have an official classification of quality wines on the lines of the 1855 system of Bordeaux. Wine judged to be the best in a given area is ranked as a *grand cru* wine and this is followed by a second category of quality which is, perhaps oddly, given the distinction of *premier cru*.

Each of Burgundy's many communes can use its own name as an appellation as can *grands crus*. *Premiers crus* can display their own name with that of the commune — for example, *Chambolle-Musigny, Pierre Dumont et Fils* — to form the appellation.

Many communes use the name of the area's most celebrated wine — *Gevrey-Chambertin*, *Puligny-Montrachet* and *Vosne-Romanée* are examples. The intention in linking the names in the first place was that lesser known and more modest wines would benefit by the association with an illustrious name and the idea has been successful.

It is important to remember that *Gevrey-Chambertin* does not come from the small and magnificent vineyard of Chambertin. Although it is a fine wine in its own right it does not rank with the splendour of *Chambertin*, which is said to have been Napoleon's favourite wine.

Basic AC wine is sold as *Bourgogne*, *Bourgogne Ordinaire* and *Bourgogne Grand Ordinaire*.

The cellars of the Domaine des Varoilles *(right)*.

RED WINES OF
BURGUNDY

A single grape, the *Pinot Noir*, is used for making the quality red wines of Burgundy, a grape which is ideally suited to the soil and climate of the region.

The most favoured district of Burgundy is the Côte d'Or which is the home of some of the most favoured wines in the world. It is a narrow strip of land, more than 25 miles long and about two and a half miles wide. Along this narrow band of land lie the many great names — Chambertin, Chambolle-Musigny, Nuits-St Georges and others.

The Côte d'Or consists of the Côtes de Nuits in the north and the Côtes de Beaune in the south.

There is a clear difference between the wines of the two *côtes*. The wine from the Côtes de Nuits is what the world understands by *Burgundy* — wine which is big, smooth, powerful in taste and bouquet. Such wines need time to achieve maturity and should not be drunk before six years at least.

The red wines of the Côtes de Beaune are lighter in character and are not quite as grand as those of the Côtes de Nuits. That is, while they are wonderful wines, they do not touch the highest levels of greatness as do some of the *Côtes de Nuits*. They are, perhaps, more refined and mature earlier than their neighbours to the north. *Alexe-Corton*, *Savigny*, *Beaune*, *Pommard* and *Volnay* are some of the great wines of the Côtes de Beaune, each contributing its own special character, asserting its own personality.

The town of Beaune is the wine capital of Burgundy, a beautiful town which is where the famous 15th century Hospice, the Hôtel-Dieu stands. Since the 15th century there has been an annual auction of wines from the vineyards of the Hospice, the proceeds of which go to the work of the Hospice, the care of the sick and old.

South of Côtes de Beaune lies Côte Chalonnaise and Maconnais. It would not be patronising to the wines of these districts to say that they are at the other end of the scale from the magnificent wines of the Côtes de Nuits. The wines of Chalonnaise are good but not much more than that. Two names are spoken of with particular respect, however: *Mercurey* and *Givry* which resemble the wines of the Côtes de Beaune.

Macon is more famous for white wine but produces a good, robust red which can be drunk young.

Beaujolais can hardly be described as *Burgundy* because, while it is made from a single grape variety, the chosen grape of *Beaujolais* is the *Gamay*, not the *Pinot Noir*.

The grape flourishes in the soil of Beaujolais producing a vast amount of wine, and it needs to as the demand for the district's wine seems almost insatiable.

The basic, light friendly wine is called *Beaujolais*. To merit this title, the wine need only contain 9 per cent alcohol. Above simple

The Clos des Varoilles *(below)*
basking in late September sunlight
has a very good micro-climate as it is
sheltered and receives the last sun of
the day.

Beaujolais *(left)* being fermented in huge vats.

Beaujolais is *Beaujolais Supérieur* which has a minimum alcohol content of 10 per cent.

There is a strong demand for *Beaujolais Primeur* or *Nouveau* in which the wine is allowed to ferment for a brief period and is available for sale soon after the harvest, officially from November 15. *Beaujolais Primeur* is a light, jolly wine, one to be gulped rather than sipped and it must be drunk fairly quickly as it has a limited life of a matter of a few months.

Beaujolais-Villages is superior to the basic *Beaujolais* and comes from a group of selected villages.

At the head of the *Beaujolais* hierarchy are the nine classic *crus* of *Beaujolais* — *Brouilly*, *Côtes de Brouilly*, *Chenas*, *Chiroubles*, *Fleurie*, *Juliénas*, *Morgon*, *Moulin-à-Vent* and *St Amour*. Each of these bears its own appellation and each has its own personality — from the silky, fragrant *Fleurie*, sometimes called the Queen of *Beaujolais*, to the firm and powerful *Moulin-à-Vent*, known as the King of *Beaujolais*. *Beaujolais* is drunk young and even these quality growths are usually drunk at three or four years, although they can age well, particularly *Juliénas* and *Moulin-à-Vent*.

WHITE WINES OF BURGUNDY

Splendid as the red wines of Burgundy are, they do not overshadow the outstanding white wines of the region.

Chablis is the best known and most available of the white *Burgundies* and is from the most northern part of the Burgundy region. As with all the quality white wines of Burgundy, it is made from a single grape variety, the *Chardonnay*, which produces a quite different wine in this green country about 100 miles south east of Paris than the southern half of the Côte d'Or where the great white *Burgundies* originate.

The typical *Chablis* is more green and more acid than its southern cousin but *Chablis* as a whole has more variety than some imagine. The *grand cru* class of *Chablis* — *Grenouilles* and *Les Clos* are two — has a pronounced richness but is very dry. The second level of quality, the *premier cru*, has a distinct style: a colour of gold with a hint of green and a firm freshness.

Below these two levels is AC *Chablis*, which accounts for most of the district's production. This is followed by *Petit Chablis* which has a lower alcohol level but can be delightful.

The best *Chablis* needs time to mature and achieve the greatness of which it is capable — a *grand cru* needs up to 10 years — but the basic *Chablis* can be drunk young, within two years.

Chablis is delightful in itself and sublime with oysters. In the 17th century it was known as 'oyster water' and is referred to by the English diarist, Samuel Pepys.

The great white wines of the Côte d'Or are to be found in the southern half of the district, the Côtes de Beaune. The principal names are *Montrachet*, *Meursalt* and *Corton-Charlemagne*.

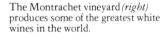

The Montrachet vineyard *(right)* produces some of the greatest white wines in the world.

The wines of Clos des Epeneaux *(above)* have great eloquence and distinction. This view of Puligny-Montrachet *(right)*, famed for its white wines, shows the gently sloping vineyards of Domaine Leflaive in the foreground.

The present owner of the Clos des Epeneaux is M le Comte Armand, here proudly displaying magnums of the great 1976 vintage in his Paris cellars *(above)*.

These pinnacles of wine are inevitably rather expensive, but there are other fine white *Burgundies* which are much more accessible — *Puligny-Montrachet*, for example, and *Chassagne-Montrachet*.

Macon produces the final truly great white wine of Burgundy, *Pouilly Fuisse*, a wine of deceptive depth and beautiful colour, green and gold with a fresh taste somewhere between *Chablis* and *Meursalt* and, like all white *Burgundies*, dry.

Less exalted wines of Macon are sold as *Macon Blanc* and *Macon Supérieure* or *Macon Villages* for those with a higher alcohol content of 11 per cent. All the white wines of Macon are made from the *Chardonnay* grape and are quality wines which, while not at the highest level of quality will not be at the highest levels of price.

An exception to the rule that the *Chardonnay* grape variety is used for white *Burgundies* is *Bourgogne Aligote* which produces a good deal of white wine for consumption at home and abroad. Because of its inferior status it is never permitted to say where it came from — it is simply *Bourgogne Aligote*, a simple, generally unremarkable wine but good value.

THE LOIRE

Even the name of the Loire has a laughing musical sound. Charm is the decription that comes into the mind most often when describing this lovely landscape of meandering rivers, green hills and fertile plains and open skies.

More than anything, the Loire region is a country of rivers. Every journey seems to be beside water, across bridges, opening up views of stretches of rivers, images of the sky and countryside reflected in the gleaming water.

The Loire itself is the longest river in France, 670 miles, rising in the Massif Central and ending its journey in the Atlantic. Feeding into this major artery are three rivers of individual character: the Cher, Indres and Vienne.

Along these rivers are the magnificent châteaux of the Loire. In this area, a château is not simply a name for an estate but the real thing; romantic manifestations of the spirit of Renaissance France, homes of kings and courts — Amboise, Azay-le-Rideau, Blois, Chenonceaux, Chambord, Usse, Villandry and others.

It is impossible to be unaware of history in the Loire as every town and village, however small, has a story to tell. It is a visual delight, stirring the imagination and the appetite for the food and wine of the Loire is exquisite. Even a fleeting visit illustrates why it was the favoured home of many French kings.

Château de la Bizoliere *(below)*, a typically charming château of the Loire Valley.

WHITE WINES OF THE LOIRE

The region is best known for its white wines and produces a range of remarkable diversity — steely and dry, fresh and fragrant, rich and sweet.

The wine growing area extends, roughly speaking, along a 200-mile stretch of the Loire, beginning with Pouilly sur Loire where the golden, smoky wine of *Pouilly-Fumé* is made.

Wine experts have repeatedly explained that *fumé* describes a smoky film that develops on the *Sauvignon* grape just before it is picked. Those who drink it remain convinced it describes the intriguing smoky flavour of the wine.

The principal districts are Sancerre, Quincy, Reuilly, Touraine, Anjou and Saumur and Muscadet.

Pouilly-Fumé is one of the most famous wines in France, and hence the world, and is consequently expensive. A great example of it is the wine of Château de Nozet-Ladoucette; a flinty, pungent wine which ages well, characteristic of good wines of the district.

On the opposite bank of the Loire is Sancerre; delightful, rolling country producing wine which is almost identical to that of Pouilly. Both are made from the *Sauvignon* grape which gives them a strong resemblance but there are specific differences.

Sancerre does not age as well and should be drunk young and fresh. Delicious as it is, it is not as distinguished as its more famous neighbour and it may be that the difference lies in the soil.

Also drunk young are the crisp, fresh wines of Quincy and Reuilly about 35 miles south-west of Sancerre. From the *Sauvignon* grape, the wine is similar to that of Sancerre but is thought to lack the character. Although not as popular, these wines are excellent examples of their kind.

Touraine is called the Garden of France; a country of prodigality, rich in everything, including wine. Touraine is the appellation of a large and productive area. Many of the wines are simple and appealing; wines to be enjoyed for their freshness and abundance. These are the wines that poets of the region, Rabelais and Ronsard, sang of and lesser men have enthusiastically agreed. There are a number of individual appellations in the Touraine district, three of which are *Touraine Amboise*, *Touraine Azay-le-Rideau* and *Touraine Mesland*. Perhaps the most telling compliment to the wine of Touraine is the fact that 80 per cent of the district's wine stays in France and is enjoyed by the natives.

The outstanding wine of the Touraine is *Vouvray*, a beautiful white wine decribed by Rabelais as 'silken'. The grape variety is the *Chinon Blanc* which is picked late when the sugar content is high. The wine produced has a high alcohol content, sometimes as much as 14 per cent. Traditionally, *Vouvray* is sweet, perfectly balanced and high in alcohol. The wine growers of Vouvray regard this kind of wine as the peak of their art but also produce fine, dry, semi-dry and sparkling wines. *Vouvray* can be drunk young but it can live to a ripe old age and there are many

Château du Nouzet-Ladoucette
(above) has 50 acres of producing
vineyard. The château itself is in
the hills above the village of Pouilly-
sur-Loire.

centenarian wines in the cellars of Vouvray, even today.

Across the river from *Vouvray* is *Montlouis*, a wine of lesser rank than *Vouvray* but delicious for all that and drunk young.

The most famous wines of Saumur — a busy, bustling town on both sides of the Loire and connected by a massive bridge — are the sparkling wines, *vin moussec* in French, which are made in the same way as *champagne*.

The main difference between them is the grape variety as *Chenin Blanc* is used for Saumur wines. Like *champagne*, the wine has a secondary fermentation in the bottle and there are strict rules about the way the wine is made. The authentic *méthode champenoise* must be followed if the wine is permitted to carry the Saumur *Appellation Controlée*.

Vast cellars have been carved out of the limestone rock and it is in these cool subterranean tunnels that the wine is made and stored. Nothing is more delightful on a hot day than to visit one of the many vineyards along the Loire and drink the cool, sparkling wine in the mouth of one of the dark, shadowy caves looking out on the river winding its course below.

Saumur is in the region of Anjou, the ancient province that was a possession of the Plantagenet kings of England for 300 years.

Anjou is best known for its rosé wines, although every kind of wine is produced in its lovely countryside. The technique of achieving the light pink wine — fresh and low in alcohol,

Baron Patrick de Ladoucette *(right)*, owner of the 50 hectare Ladoucette domain.

refreshing on summer days — originated here. The colour comes from a brief period when the skins are left with the grape juice, a matter of a few hours, which imparts the distinctive colour and gives the wine its freshness.

About a quarter of Anjou's wine production is *Rosé d'Anjou*, the best of which is *Rosé de Cabernet*, made from the *Cabernet Franc*, which is fuller and stronger than simple *Rosé d'Anjou*.

The district also produces some splendid sweet white wines under the general name of *Coteaux de Layon*. The *Chenin Blanc* grape is used and the wine is made in the same way as *Sauternes*, the grape being picked late and when they are affected by the condition, *pourriture noble* or noble rot.

The outstanding wines of this kind are *Quart de Chaumes* and *Bonnenzeau*; sweet, fruity yet elegant wines that can outlive even the great wines of Sauternes. Ten years is usually the least time allowed for maturing and 25 is often better.

Anjou also produces a small amount of dry white wine, the best of which carries the Savennières appellation. The *Chenin* grape variety is used and the resulting wine can be marvellously complex; often starting life as typically dry but maturing to honeyed fruitiness. An example of the greatest of this wine comes from the Château de la Bizolière.

As the Loire approaches the Atlantic, it passes through the Muscadet district. *Muscadet* is used to decribe the area although it is the name of the grape used for the district's famous wines.

The wine of Muscadet is unique: pale, almost clear, very dry with a hint of the sea in its astringent flavour. The wine is usually drunk young, within a year or two of bottling. The best, most authentic *Muscadet* flavour is found in the wine made '*sur lie*'. In this method the wine is left to mature in one barrel, rather than being transferred from one barrel to another, as is the usual practice, to remove the wine's deposits. *Muscadet* of this kind is fresh, crisp, incisive, ideal for drinking with shellfish, as the good people of Brittany know well.

Below the level of quality of *Apellation Controllée* is the VDQS of the district, *Gros Plant*, which is a grape producing a sharper wine with more edge. It is not considered as fine as *Muscadet* but enjoyed by those who like its distinctive flavour.

RED WINES OF THE LOIRE

Although famous for white wine, the Loire produces a variety of red wines. Most of these are pleasant, simple, quaffing wines of no great distinction but there are one or two worth special attention. The best red wine comes from the vineyards on the banks of the Vienne, that graceful tributary of the Loire. At Chinon and Bourgeuil, the *Cabernet Franc* grape variety produces some fine wines: beautiful in colour, fruity but dry in the mouth with a full, fragrant bouquet. Each wine has its devotees. Some say *Chinon* is fuller in flavour and has a bouquet reminiscent of violets while others claim *Bourgeuil* is superior, living longer in the bottle and having a hint of wild raspberries in the bouquet.

Wine apart, Chinon is the more favoured of the two places, standing beside a serene stretch of the Vienne below the golden château where Joan of Arc met the French court. Bourgeuil, in contrast, is notable for its nuclear power station.

RHÔNE

Wine has been made in the Rhône valley for as long as anywhere in France. Six centuries before the birth of Christ, Greeks from Asia Minor established the port of Massilia in what is now Marseilles. They were traders and wine was among the things they traded. From Massilia they explored the country north, along the great river Rhône, spreading the gospel of wine.

Today, the Rhône Valley is one of the greatest producers of wine in France; an average 35,200,000 gallons a year of red, white and rosé from the 125-mile river valley between Lyon and Avignon. The range of wine is enormous: from rare and expensive to robust and inexpensive.

There are two quite distinct and separate parts of the Côtes du Rhône. the northern and southern zones. The wine from these two regions is quite different as different grape varieties are used and different soil conditions exist in the two areas. In general, the best wines come from the northern part of the Rhône valley.

RED WINES OF THE
CÔTES DU RHÔNE

The *Syrah* grape is used for the red wines of the north, a grape that produces wine of great power and deep colour, reputed to have originated in Persia.

Among the most celebrated wines of the area is *Côtes Rôtie*, although the production is fairly small and most of the wine is enjoyed by the discerning population of France. The vines grow on steep granite hills and are literally 'roasted' by the sun. High in tannin and alcohol, this big, powerful wine needs time to mature, from four to five years.

South of *Côtes Rôtie* are the vineyards of Hermitage, the oldest in France, established by Gaspard de Stérimberg in the early years of the 13th century who built a chapel high on the hillside which stands today.

The big red wines of Hermitage develop a soft and velvety character as they mature. One of the greatest is the *Hermitage la Chappelle* from the house of Paul Jaboulet Ainé.

The *Syrah* grape variety is the major influence on the red wines of Crose-Hermitage, splendid wines but of lesser quality than the noble Hermitage. They mature more quickly and more is produced. The reds of Saint-Joseph and Cornas are also worth seeking out.

The southern zone of the Côtes du Rhône is a much larger wine-growing area which extends beyond the river valley and produces about 85 per cent of all Côtes du Rhône wine.

Soil conditions are different; the shallow slopes have a lighter sandy and chalk soil, often covered with large stones, up to three feet in depth in some places. Unlike the northern zone, a number of grape varieties is used for different wines — six or seven in most cases but the renowned Châteauneuf-du-Pape has no less than 13 grape varieties.

The village of Châteauneuf-du-Pape takes its name from the new castle built for the Pope when the Papal court was moved from the intrigues of Rome to the peace of Avignon in 1309.

The wine is blessed — rich in colour, powerful, balanced, high in alcohol, from 12 to 14 per cent. The secret of its power may come from the long exposure of the vines to the sun and the high temperatures that the vines experience. The large stones covering the soil of the vineyard absorb the heat of the sun in the day and reflect it on the vines at night.

Near Châteauneuf-du-Pape is Gigondas, where a similar wine is produced: dark in colour, spicy bouquet with perhaps even more body.

A number of villages are permitted to use the appellation *Côtes du Rhône Villages*. They are good, honest red wines made from a number of grape varieties of which the *Grenache* is the best known. The villages of this appellation include Vinsobres, Rochegude, Saint-Pantaléon, Rousset, Valreas, Cairanne, Rasteau and Vacueyras.

At the end of the southern district of the Côtes du Rhône are the wines of Coteaux du Triscastin, Côtes de Ventous and Côtes du Luberon. The first two are AC wines, the latter VDQS wines but all are good, well balanced with a powerful bouquet.

WHITE WINES OF THE CÔTES DU RHÔNE

The white wine production of Côtes du Rhône is much less than that of red wine but it includes some fine wines, including France's rarest white wine from Château Grillet, a vineyard of less than three hectares.

Few people are likely to have the opportunity to drink this full, scented wine, any more than they are likely to sample the similar white wine from nearby Condrieu from a vineyard of only 10 hectares.

The classic white wines of the northern part of the Côtes du Rhône are from Hermitage. These are made from the *Marsanne* grape variety and benefit from long maturity, developing great power and body as they develop. Traditionally Hermitage wines would need up to 10 years before drinking but the wines are now made to be drunk earlier. *Saint-Peray* is a lovely white wine, similar to *Hermitage* and from the same grape varieties. Saint-Peray also produces sparkling wine as does the vineyard of Clairette de Die to the south.

A vineyard planted with Chenin grapes *(left)*.

The white wines of the southern zone are pleasant, quite powerful and usually dry but they lack the distinction of those from the north. The appellation *Côtes du Rhône Villages* is a guarantee of quality.

The southern Rhône's greatest light wine is the famous rosé, especially of Tavel, Lirac, Chusclan, Laudun and Saint-Gervais. These wines are to be enjoyed when young and fresh, light and delicious on summer days.

CHAMPAGNE

Some wines may be drunk in solitude, quietly appreciated for their subtlety and discretion. *Champagne* is not one of these; it is a wine to be shared, celebrated, a wine of joy.

There is only one authentic *champagne*. Indeed, *champagne* is an *Appellation d'Origine Controlée* in its own right. It is grown in a strictly defined area, the centre of which is the ancient city of Reims. The four principal wine growing areas are the Montagne de Reims; the Vallée de la Marne; the Côtes de Blancs and the Aube vineyards.

Vines have been grown in the region since Roman times but the method of producing *champagne* was not discovered until the 17th century when Dom Pérignon, who was in charge of the cellar at the abbey of Hautvillers, discovered a method of controlling the secondary fermentation that occurred in his wines.

Although on a northerly latitude for vines, the Champagne region has warm summers and dry autumns and it also has soil conditions which are ideal for vines — chalk covered with a thin layer of limestone.

The grape varieties are the white *Chardonnay*, the red *Pinot Noir* and the red *Meuninier*. Some 75 per cent of the Champagne vineyards grow red grapes and most *champagne* is a blend of red and white grapes. Where the wine is made exclusively from white grapes, it carries the title *Blanc de Blancs*.

Champagne is usually made from grapes of different years, but when the harvest is exceptionally good the wine may be made of grapes of that year only, thereby producing a '*millesime*' or vintage wine.

The secret of *champagne* is the way it is made. Important as the growing and picking of the grapes are, the real art of *champagne* is in the making and blending of the wines.

The original stages of the wine making are the same as for other wines; the difference is the secondary fermentation which takes place in the bottle. These bottles are stored in a labyrinthine spread of tunnels deep in the heart of the chalky subsoil throughout the region. In this period the sugar is converted into alcohol and carbonic acid is created, forming the tiny bubbles which are the hallmark of *champagne*.

The bubbles in the fermentation vat
for red grapes *(below)* show the
carbon dioxide produced during
fermentation.

Non-vintage *champagne* must be left for at least a year from the completion of the secondary fermentation and most are kept for two years or more. Vintage *champagne* is stored for three or more years.

The secondary fermentation causes the formation of deposits which stick to the side of the bottle. This deposit is collected in the neck of the bottle in a time-honoured method. The bottles are racked with the necks tilted downwards slightly. Each bottle is individually turned daily for several weeks — *'remuage'* as it is called — and the bottle is gradually placed upside down.

After the *remuage* comes the *'dégorgement'* in which the deposits are removed. The neck of the bottle is frozen, the cork removed and the pressure ejects the frozen deposits.

The small amount of wine lost is replaced by the *'dosage'* a mixture of sugar and wine which determines whether the *champagne* will be very dry, dry, medium sweet or sweet. *Brut* is the traditional term for the driest *champagne*. *Sec* (literally dry) means slightly sweet and *demi-sec* means sweet.

ALSACE

Alsace is in north west France, bordering Germany, between the Vosges and Rhine rivers. Its geographical position and its history give the region a unique style. It was part of Germany from 1870 to 1918 and there are echoes of the German influence in the language, architecture and wine.

The grape varieties are the same as those used in Germany and the climate is similar, but the wine has a character of its own; a combination of German quality with a dash of Gallic finesse.

The wines of Alsace are unusual among French wines in that they are named after the grape from which they are made rather than their place of origin, which is a matter of such fierce pride in other wine growing areas.

The grape is all-important: in every bottle of Alsatian wine the grape can be tasted. Simplicity and naturalness are characteristics of the wine which is made in the traditional manner; stored in casks for several months, transferred to clean casks and finally bottled.

The wines produced by the different grape varieties are: *Riesling* (the king of Alsatian wines; a dry white wine with an unusually full bouquet); *Sylvaner* (light dry white wine, best drunk young); *Gewurztztraminer* (a heady, fruity white wine with a powerful musky bouquet); *Pinot Blanc* (dry white, well balanced); *Pinot Gris* or *Tokay d'Alsace* (fine fruity full bodied wine but no relation to the famous *Tokay* of Hungary); *Muscat d'Alsace* (dry and fruity white wine with the distinctive flavour of *Muscat* grapes); *Pinot Noir* or *Rosé d'Alsace* is an exception to the usual white wines of Alsace as it is a rosé wine — dry, fruity and refreshing.

Alsace wines are bottled in tall, green bottles like those of Moselle. They should be drunk young but the finest can age.

Edelzwicker is the term used for wine made from the approved or noble grape varieties (*Edel* means noble) and *Zwicker* describes wine made from ordinary grape varieties — it is this wine that is quaffed in such quantities by Alsatians as part of their everyday life.

The Gewurztraminer does very well on the steep slopes found in some parts of Alsace *(right)*. It achieves great ripeness thanks to the excellent exposure to the sun.

A combination of new and old oak barrels *(above)*. Some wine-makers feel that in some years the character of the vintage needs new oak more than the others.

Young vines *(above)* are protected with plastic from frost or animals. This practice is ideal in a very dry climate, but is not always desirable in wetter climates as humidity can build up under the plastic and damage the vines.

OTHER WINE AREAS OF FRANCE

Wine is produced in almost every *département* of France, apart from the extreme north and along the damp Channel coast. All of it is good; some is excellent and a just cause of local pride.

Jura and Savoie in the mountainous region of eastern France produce interesting white wines, especially the straw wine of Jura which is made from grapes picked in November, spread on straw to dry and pressed in February. The result is a wine of great alcohol strength which is quite unique.

In the south east there are the vineyards of Provence, the oldest in France. These are best known for excellent rosé wines but there are also good quality reds and a lesser quantity of dry white wines under the *Appellation Controlée* Côtes de Provence.

Languedoc Roussillon, west of Provence, is the largest producer of wine in France and provides most of the country's *vins de pays* as well as good ADC and VDQS wines. *Appellation controlée* wines include *Côtes du Roussillon* and *Roussillon Villages* (which must have an alcohol content of at least 12 per cent); Fitou; *Blanquette de Limoux* (a sparkling wine); *Faugères*, *Saint-Chinian*, *Minervois* and *Coteaux de Languedoc*.

The VDQS wines of the region are every bit as good as the AC wines, according to experts, and they are also somewhat cheaper. *Corbières* and *Costières du Gard* are good wines, most of them red but with some dry white.

The south west has a great variety of wine, apart from the riches of Bordeaux. The red and white wines of Bergerac are very good and some — such as the sweet white *Monbazillac* — are great wines in any company.

Côtes du Frontonnais produces sound red wines and Cahors produces some good value reds. The most famous wine of the south west is *Jurançon*, from the mountainous region south of Pau, in the shadow of the mighty Pyrenees. The wine is sweet, mellow, rich and ages well. The local growers are now making a dry version of *Jurançon* which is a delightful companion on an al fresco meal in the hills with local cheese and sausages.

ITALY

Dr Biondi Santi — owner of the Biondi Santi estate — holding a bunch of Sangiovese Grosso grapes *(above)*.

Italy is the leading wine producing country in the world, well ahead of France which comes second. It has an almost bewildering variety of wine but a common approach to it: a natural, uninhibited enjoyment of wine and, indeed, all the pleasures of life. It is not noticeable for grand, aristocratic wines but is a country of many good and some great wines.

Because the climate is predictable, the wine of Italy does not differ greatly from one year to another, certainly not as much as in other countries, apart from some of the greatest Italian wines. The year on the bottle is generally no more than an indication of how long the wine has been made, useful in the case of wine which requires ageing, rather than identifying the greatness or otherwise of a specific year. The wine grower in Germany, for example, may produce wine in one year in almost impossible conditions which will be reflected in the quality of the wine, making it quite different from the wine of a more favoured year.

In Italy, the climate is beneficial for the vine and the making of wine seems natural, almost inevitable.

Wine has been made in Italy for some 3000 years and was introduced by those energetic evangelists of the Ancient World, the Greeks. The history of wine and viticulture is well chronicled in Roman literature, in the works of historians and the songs of poets. Then, as now, good wines were honoured. One of the most famous was *Falerian* — the poet Martial wrote of wanting to 'kiss lips moist with old *Falerian*' — which probably came from an area near Naples where wine of the same name is still produced.

Wine growing and wine making were carefully studied with proper attention given to such questions as grape varieties and soil conditions. Columella observed elegantly: 'that wine is immeasurably the best which needs only its own nature to give pleasure'.

The observation has lost nothing of its truth over the centuries, and it may represent a tradition which survives today and is expressed in the rule that no Italian wine may be chaptalized (when the alcohol content of wine is increased by adding sugar during fermentation) as is allowed in Germany and France.

Today, wine is produced in each of the country's 19 regions. It is a wine-growing land of infinite variety and immense size, stretching from the Alps to Sicily with thousands of vineyards, more than a hundred grape varieties contributing to the rich variety of its wines.

Above everything, Italians are individuals and very much so in their wine growing methods. Even today there are small peasant farmers producing wine in a way that has hardly changed for centuries who exist alongside large, sophisticated systems employed by co-operatives in which growers have suppressed their individuality to produce wines of a consistent standard.

The acceptance of common standards is fairly new in Italy, though controls have existed for many years in some areas, such as Tuscany.

Biondi Santi place much emphasis on the quality of the grapes in their wines, only using the very best for the estate wine. These newly picked Sangiovese Grosso grapes *(above)* are in excellent condition.

This area at Vicchiomaggio *(left)* is an example of a specialized vineyard. A specialized vineyard is devoted solely to vines rather than, as was the custom in much of Italy, mixing grape growing with the cultivation of other crops such as olives.

The grape pickers set off to start the vintage *(right)*.

In times past, the Italian wine grower simply produced wine to be drunk. If the label was not completely accurate, well, it was still wine and there was plenty of it.

A change in the approach to indentifying wine and the reputation of Italian wine came in 1963 with the introduction of new wine laws. These are similar to the *Appellation Controlée* of France and give three levels of quality.

Denominazione Semplice is basic wine, equivalent to French *vin de table* or German *Tafelwein*. The second and most useful level is the *Denominazione di Origine Controllata* (DOC) which ensures the wine is produced in a defined area, is made from approved grape varieties, is aged and bottled according to certain rules and has a minimum alcohol content.

The third and highest level of quality is *Denominazione Controllata e Garantita* in which wines from specific estates must meet strict rules governing place of origin, the name of the bottler and the grower, the alcohol content and the size of container in which the wine may be sold. The DOCG is a rare distinction at present but more wines are likely to achieve it as outstanding wines emerge from the ranks of the DOC. There are now more than 200 DOC Italian wines, which is an indication of how successful the new wine laws are. Since their introduction there has been a dramatic improvement in the overall quality of Italian wine and a massive increase in the export of Italian wines.

The idiosyncrasies of Italian wine labelling can be confusing. Very often, the grape variety from which the wine is made will be given prominence; but the main identification might be the village or district where the wine originated or it might have a single name such as *Lacrima Christi*. For example, Barolo is a place name and the great red wine which carries this name is made

The Biondi Santi estate *(below)*
surrounds the modest family house.

These Sangiovese grapes *(right)* have just been harvested.

from the *Nebbiolo* grape variety, but *Nebbiolo* is also used to describe wine made from the grape but not in Barolo. However, once the principal grape varieties and wine areas are known, the problem largely disappears.

— RED WINES OF ITALY —

The 19 regions of Italy produce just about every conceivable kind of wine; a diversity unmatched by any country. Red wines of every description and shade are produced.

Piedmont in the far north west of Italy is among the country's most successful regions as far as quality wine is concerned. It is a vast area with the city of Turin at its centre and the best wine comes from the mountainous country to the north; some of the best wines grow at 2000 feet and more above sea level. To the north it is protected by the Alps, prettily described by one wine writer as being like a sunny south-facing balcony.

The region produces two of the greatest red wines in Italy; *Barolo* and *Barbaresco*. These are full, powerful wines which share something of the character of the Côtes du Rhône; Piedmont is on the same latitude as the leading wine growing

Grapes from the Campo Fiorin vineyard *(right)* are used to make the non-DOC red wine which has brought the Masi estate to the attention of the world.

Dr Sandro Boscaini *(above)* is the head of the Masi firm. His family have run the estate since the eighteenth century.

areas of the Rhône Valley. They are made from the *Nebbiolo* grape; a truly great grape producing memorable wines of power and fragrance. The name comes from the Italian word for mist, presumably because the grapes are picked late in the year when autumn mists are common.

Barolo is considered the greater of the two because it ages even longer and has a little more body. Both wines are aged for at least three years in cask before bottling. The greatest examples of *Nebbiolo* wines are from Barolo and Barbaresco — both are village names — but there are other good wines with local names. When the wine is simply styled *Nebbiolo* or *Nebbiolo Piedmontese*, it is an indication that the wine, though made from the great grape variety, comes from an area that is not highly rated.

Barbera is the most prolific grape variety in Piedmont and produces big, powerful wines. The best known are from Barbera d'Asti and others which carry the name of the grape with a district name. Good red wines of Piedmont known by the grape variety from which they are made include *Friesa*, *Dolcetto* and *Grignolino*.

The best wines of the Veneto region are centred around Verona, the city of Romeo and Juliet where even the wines have a Shakespearian ring. Consider the mellifluous *Valpolicella*, for

These Merlot vines are planted vertically to the slope *(below)*. This is the conventional method. However, the main concern with all vine planting is to ensure maximum exposure to the sun. The nets are put over the vines if hail seems imminent.

The river Isonzo *(above)* is on the border of Collio with the Grave del Friuli area. These white Sauvignon grapes *(right)* are trained high. They produce a dry white wine which is crisp and fragrant.

These rows of Tocai *(above)* are planted horizontally to the slope. It is more usual to plant the vines vertically to the slope, but this configuration gives better exposure to the sun on this site.

example, with its beautiful red colour, round taste and fragrant bouquet. It is one of Italy's best known wines and is made from *Corvina*, *Negrara* and *Molinara* grape varieties as is *Bardolino* (surely a drinking companion of Falstaff's) which is a good deal lighter than *Valpolicella* or *Valpantena*, almost identical to *Valpolicella* and from the same grapes.

Although a considerable producer of wine, Lombardy is not the force it once was. The most distinguished red wines come from the Valtinella region, near Lake Como. Some of the finest are *Sassella*, *Grumello* and *Inferno*. They are made from the noble *Nebbiolo* grape variety but not exclusively and are consequently not as fine or as full as the great wines made only from *Nebbiolo*, such as *Barolo*.

Trentino and Alto Adige are mountainous regions where the vines are perched on narrow terraces high above sea level. Among the best known red wines are *Teroldego*, *Caldaro* and the fuller *Santa Madalena*.

Friuli-Venelia-Giulia in the north east against the border with Yugoslavia is something of an oddity in that, while the region has strong historical associations with Austria and Hungary, the major influence in the vineyards is French with the *Cabernet* variety producing big red wines and the *Gamay* of Beaujolais responsible for the wines of high alcohol content.

The rolling hills of the Collio area *(above)* are ideal for wine growing. It is an old established wine growing area. This small DOC is considered the best area in Friuli-Venezia-Giulia because of its terrain and slopes.

Emilia-Romagna is more renowned for its cuisine than its wine but has some good red wine which can be drunk young or given time to age from the *Sangiovese* grape variety and the distinctive *Lambrusco* which is dry, red and sparkling. Opinions vary about this unusual wine which froths out of the bottle and has a pronounced prickle in the taste, but it is said to be perfect with the local speciality of pigs' trotters.

Chianti is the best known Italian wine. Indeed, it has come to symbolize Italian wines throughout the world. A beautiful wine from a beautiful part of Tuscany, between Florence and Siena, it is rather unusal.

First, it is made from a combination of black and white grapes — *Sangiovese*, *Canaiolo*, *Malvais* and the white *Trebbiano*. The popular, fresh prickly taste comes from the *'governo'* method in which a secondary fermentation is produced, after the first natural fermentation, by adding a mixture of rich, dried grapes. The *'governo'* is usually added to *Chianti* wines which are to be drunk early. Wine destined for longer maturity is fermented in the natural way and bottled in conventional bottles of Bordeaux shape and usually carries the description *'reserva'*. The well-known

The Muscat grape *(above)*, backbone of Italy's most famous sparkling wine, *Asti Spumante*.

straw-covered *Chianti* flasks indicate a young, fresh wine intended to be drunk young.

There is a world of difference between the lively youngster of the straw-covered flask and the deeper-coloured, fuller character of *Chianti* that has aged for eight years or so.

Chianti Classico is the best *Chianti* and is produced in a defined number of communes of the original area where *Chianti* was produced. Wine made from the same grape varieties in the same way in nearby districts may be — and is — very good but is only permitted the description *Chianti* without the *classico*.

Tuscany produces many other agreeable wines, apart from *Chianti*, and one that can be mentioned in the same breath is *Brunello di Montacello*, a single grape variety made from the *Sangiovese*, like *Chianti*, but without the additions of other grapes. The wine has a reputation for longevity, up to 50 years in bottle according to some experts. It is aged or five or six years in casks before being bottled. A big, powerful wine, it is often said to be Italy's *Burgundy* but the comparison is not a good one as it should be opened for 24 hours before serving.

The best of Italy's wine comes from the north of the country. The further south one travels, the more coarse the wines — especially the reds — become, with a few isolated exceptions. Yet, an enormous amount of wine is produced in the south, especially in Apulia, forming the heel of Italy, which is the leading wine producing region of Italy. Most of its wine is used for blending and finds its way north in tankers out of Brindisi.

Sicily has strong, fierce wines and is probably best known for *Marsala*, a fortified wine, like sherry and port, which can live to a ripe old age, but there are good wines from Corvo and Etna.

— WHITE WINES OF ITALY —

The white wines of Italy are almost as diverse as the red wines. Again, the wines tend to be good and plentiful rather than outstanding, but many are excellent.

Piedmont in the northwest of Italy is essentially red wine country but it is also the home of Italy's most famous sparkling wine, *Asti Spumante*, made from *muscat* grapes. Most of it is sweet and delicate. The method of production is not usually that followed in the making of French *champagne*, but there are a few exceptions for a superior example of the breed, as the *champenoise méthode* is lengthy and costly. The grapes are fermented in closed vats and bottled under pressure, producing a cheery, bubbly wine which is ideal for celebrations.

Piedmont is also the centre of the *vermouth* industry. *Vermouth* is a fortified wine; the wine enhanced by the addition of mountain herbs. The tradition of herb-flavoured wines, often with medicinal properties, goes back to Greek times although the making of *vermouth* in Piedmont dates from the 18th century. The main styles are a spicy red; a sweet white and a dry white.

Castle Vicchiomaggio *(above)* high
on a hill above Greve, the centre of
the Chianti Classico area.

Perhaps the greatest triumph of the Veneto is the white wine of
Soave, for many the finest white wine in Italy — dry, smooth, with
no trace of acidity, clear in colour and thoroughly refreshing. It
should be drunk as young as possible.

There's a strong echo of Alsace in the white wines of Trentino-
Alto Adige and the grape varieties show the influence of
Germany, especially in the German-speaking Alto Adige, where
Riesling, *Gewurztraminer*, *Müller Thurgau* and *Sylvaner* are
grown.

As might be expected, the wine growers of the Italian-speaking
Trentino favour Italian grapes. *Vernaccia* and *Nosiala* are two of
the most popular, producing wine of the same name.

In Friuli, in the north east, the French grape varieties are
popular. *Sauvignon* is widely grown and produces some fine
wines. There is also *Tocai*, a dry white wine, which is no relation
of the famous *Tokay* of Hungary but a local grape variety. The
Piccolit sweet dessert wine made from semi-dried grapes of the
same name, is the pride of the region and has even been likened to
Château d'Yquem.

The popular *Trebbiano* grape is widely grown in the Emilia-
Romagna regions and makes first class dry white wine. The sweet
white *Albana* is much enjoyed by the citzens of Bologna and is
notable for its high alcohol content.

There is a white *Chianti* but it is in no way comparable with the
red. The outstanding white wine of Tuscany is *Vernaccia si San
Gimignano*, a dry gentle wine made near Siena from the
Vernaccia grape.

The best white wines of Italy are found in the middle region of
the country. *Orvieto* is the major contribution of Umbria, a fine
white wine from the *Trebbiano* grape which is made sweet and

The beautiful Badia di Coltibuono
(above).

dry; both are excellent.

The volcanic rock of the region gives the wine of Orvieto a subtle distinction, a hint of bitterness under the pleasing freshness. The sweet *Orvieto Abbocato* is highly regarded. Made from grapes which ferment in deep caves in the volcanic rock, often for as long as three years, the sweetness comes from the addition of the juice of dried grapes during fermentation. The resulting wine is never richly sweet but has a light, sweet, delicate character. *Verdicchio* is an excellent dry white wine from the Adriatic and is made of the grape of the same name.

One of the most intriguing wine names in Italy — a country where the names of wines often have an operatic flavour — is *Est Est Est*. The chief claim to fame of this dry or sweet white wine is the name which originates in the fondness for wine of Bishop John Fugger who, in 1110, was travelling south to Rome. As a sensible precaution, a servant went ahead to ensure that accommodation, food and wine in the inns ahead was suitable for his master.

Approved establishments were indicated by the word Est on the door. When the servant arrived in Montefiascone he was so impressed or influenced by the local wine that he gave it a three star rating, scribbling Est Est Est on the door. The enthusiasm of the servant was shared by his master for Bishop Fugger never reached Rome. He stayed in Montefiascone, sampling the local wine, and is buried in the village churchyard.

Castelli Romani is the name of an enchanting district in the Alban hills, south of Rome and wines bearing this description come from a strictly defined area. The wines are white, dry or sweet, and delicious with the excellent food of the region.

The most famous of the *vini dei castelli romani* is *Frascati*, a village whose wine is sweet or dry but the dry is the better of the two, firm, positive, not acidic. Other good *castelli* wines are *Montecompatri*, *Marino* and *Colonna*.

North of Naples is the ancient name of Falernum, a dry but full white wine which may or may not be the great wine of ancient times (as some experts believe that was actually red).

White wine of any quality scarcely exists south of Naples but there are several good, refreshing whites from Ravello and there is the well known *Lacrima Christi*, a white wine from the slopes of Mount Vesuvius which is said to have derived its name from the tears Jesus Christ wept on seeing that human wickedness flourished even in a place as beautiful as the Bay of Naples.

Many Italian estates are still family based. The grapes are often harvested by the estate workers and their families or other local people *(below)*.

On some estates the capsules for the bottles are still put on by hand *(below)*.

At Biondi Santi a small hand press *(below)* is used in preference to a mechanical one. This is so that the grapes are only pressed very lightly.

GERMANY

The chapel at Kloster Eberbach *(above)*, scene of famous wine tastings, wine fairs and wine auctions.

German wine is a triumph in a very real sense because the German wine grower faces problems unknown to growers in most other parts of Europe. The main problems are to do with climate; severe winters and unpredictable summers mean that the grapes do not fully ripen and are low in essential sugar content.

Yet these difficulties have not disheartened growers as wine has been made in Germany since Roman times and the German wine industry produces wines which are acclaimed and sought after throughout the world. The overwhelming majority of German wines are white and notable for their lightness and freshness. They are generally less alcoholic than the wines of, say, France but alcoholic strength is not as important in German wine as it is in French.

This is a fundamental difference between the two countries. In France, the level of alcohol is an intrinsic part of the *Appellation Controlée*. In Germany, the level of alcohol is not as important as the correct balance between acidity and sweetness. Delicacy and fragrance are the prized qualities.

Given the vagaries of the climate, it is obvious that the grapes do not always have the natural sugar content to provide the necessary level of alcohol or to give the touch of fruitiness that is the prized characteristic of German wine. This deficiency is made up by the addition of sugar to increase the alcohol level and give the required level of sweetness.

The importance of sweetness in German wines is demonstrated by the fact that the assessment of quality is based on the natural sweetness of the grape juice.

Unlike France, the basic assessment of quality does not recognize the superiority of one wine region over another. Every wine is judged at the beginning of its life on natural sugar content by what is called the Oechsle system.

In theory, any German wine may achieve the highest level of quality, if it is able to produce grapes with the required sugar content. In practice, of course, the same vineyards tend to produce the quality wine because they have the necessary conditions of climate, soil, grape variety and skill. The names of the leading growers are important for the buyer because they are an indication of the quality of the wine but they have no bearing on the basic assessment of quality.

There are 11 wine-growing regions in Germany which are divided into two or more *Bereiche* (district). A *Bereich* will include a number of villages and will often take its name from the best-known village of the area. Each *Bereich* is made up of a collection of vineyards, called a *Grosslagen*, and a single vineyard is known as *Einzellagen*. Obviously, the level of quality of the wine may vary in the broader appellations and will be more consistent in the more precise names.

The categories of German wine are the basic *Tafelwein* (table wine); *Landwein* (land wine), which comes from one of a number of approved regions, and *Qualitätswein* (quality wine).

Care in the vineyards during
vinification and the hand of master
wine-makers ensure the continuing
quality of German wines *(below)*.

In these ancient cellars there are several sizes of cask *(above)*. The small ones are most important for making the small quantities of late harvest wines.

Quality wines are divided into two classes: QbA (*Qualitätswein Bestimmter Anbaugebiete*) quality wine from a named area which is made from approved grape varieties and to which sugar has been added; QmP (*Qualitätswein mit Prädikat*) quality wine with special attributes, which is the finest wine to which sugar has not been added.

Testing of these quality wines is rigorous. QbA and QmP wines undergo a three-stage examination before being given an approved testing number which must appear on the bottle. From the number, the origin of the wine can be traced at any time. The first of the examinations is the testing for ripeness at harvest time which is measured in Oechsle degrees and gives the natural sugar content of the grape juice. This assessment is made by independent officials who make random checks.

Testing for ripeness is followed by further checks on the finished wine in the laboratory where alcohol content, residual sugar and acidity levels are measured.

Finally, the wine is tasted by independent wine officials who judge the wine on its merits and who do not know the identity of the grower. In addition to these indications of quality, German wine labels will often carry a seal or award. These awards are for superior quality wines which are given recognition in the form of bronze, silver or gold prizes: bronze is good, silver is better and gold is excellent.

The Kurfürstenhof banner *(above)*, one of the most famous names in German wine.

This picture *(left)* shows wine tasting in the Cabinet cellar of the Kloster Eberbach in 1847. It was the Duke of Nassau who first took to using this cellar for keeping the best quality wines. The term *Kabinett* was first used for the 1811 Steinberger.

QmP is the highest level of quality for German wines and has six categories, based on ripeness at harvest.

Kabinett: dry elegant wines with a touch of fruitiness but low in alcohol.

Spätlese: literally 'late harvest' because the grapes are gathered after the normal harvest to allow them to reach a high degree of ripeness. The wine is balanced and well rounded.

Auslese: wine of intense bouquet and taste, richer than *Spätlese*. The grapes are left on the vine to ripen and are picked in individual bunches.

Beerenauslese: an exquisite, luscious wine made from grapes affected by the 'noble rot' fungus and picked by hand.

Trockenbeerenauslese: the greatest of German wines, made from individual grapes that have been allowed to shrivel and dry and have a very high sugar content. Beautiful, sweet as honey but expensive.

Eiswein (ice wine) is another rare and expensive wine. Grapes of *Beerenauslese* quality are left on the vine and harvested when the juice of the grapes is frozen. The grapes are pressed in this state which gives the juice a high concentration of natural sugar. The method is risky because if the weather does not turn cold enough the grapes simply wither on the vines.

The 11 wine growing regions of Germany are Rheingau; Rheinhessen; Rheinpfalz; Mosel-Saar-Ruwer; Mittelrhein; Ahr; Baden; Wurttemberg; Franken; Nahe and Hessige Bergstrasse.

R H E I N G A U

The topsoil in the vineyard of Rudesheim *(above)* is extremely stony.

The Rheingau is Germany's most beautiful wine country, an idyllic stretch of country alongside some 20 miles of the Rhine when the south to north journey of the river is interrupted by a brief diversion westwards beside the Taunus hills.

The Rhine is majestically broad here and the sun is reflected from its waters on to the southern-facing slopes where the wines grow. It has what is probably the mildest climate in Germany, a climate that is responsible for the way the vines flourish and the production of some of Germany's greatest wines.

It is the home of the king of grapes, the *Riesling*: a grape variety of nobility but demanding about the conditions in which it will grow. The Rheingau provides these conditions; south facing slopes, a constant amount of sunshine and soil which contains the subtle elements necessary to give the wine character and even greatness.

The *Riesling* is a remarkable grape with a distinctive and powerful bouquet of flowers. It has had time to become accustomed to life in the Rheingau as it was brought to the region by Hildegard, abbess of the convent near Rudesheim, in the 12th century. In the Middle Ages the church was involved in the cultivation of vines, originally to provide wine for its services as wine was an important symbolic element in the rituals of the

The village of Nierstein can be seen behind the Rehbach vineyard on the Rheinfront *(left)*.

Vintaging is taking place in the Avelsbach vineyard *(right)*. The small plastic receptacles ensure that the grapes are not crushed by their own weight. The steepness of the vineyards can also be seen in the background.

church, and subsequently as an important source of revenue.

The Benedictine order was traditionally associated with wine growing throughout Europe. Monks from the same order tended the vines at Johannisberg and were involved in one of the greatest discoveries of viticulture in 1775. Like many leaps forward in human knowledge it was accidental.

At that time, the grape harvest could not begin without the permission of the bishop who would make his decision after examining a sample of the year's grapes. In 1775 the grape sample was duly despatched but the messenger failed to return. History is a little uncertain about the reasons, but illness and capture by brigands are given as possible causes.

The monks waited as time passed and the grapes shrivelled on the vines and started to show signs of rot. At last, in desperation, they decided to proceed with the harvest, making what they could of what seemed to be a disaster. However, when the wine was tasted, it was a revelation: full, heavy, golden with a perfume of honey and fruit.

It was the first example of wine being made from grapes with the condition 'noble rot' or *botrytis cinerea* and the wine was the first *Trockenbeerenauslese*, which is the pinnacle of German wine making. Since that time, the best German wines have been made from late picked grapes. *Trockenbeerenauslese* wine is expensive — noble rot appears perhaps once in every four years — but it is unique.

This painted cask head *(below)* shows the Seip family crest. The Kurfürstenhof estate came into the Seip family in 1950.

Anno 1696

Familienwappen

90

Harvesting *(below)* is in progress at Johannisberg. The distance between the top and bottom of the rows is approximately 260 metres.

The banks of the broad and busy river in the Rheingau are dotted with famous wine towns such as Rudeheim, Mittelheim, Oestrich Erbach and Geisenheim, home of the German Wine Institute. Just in the region is Hochheim, the town which provides the word *hock*, the English name for white Rhine wines. It was at Hochheim that Queen Victoria had shown a liking for wines from the village.

Although there are many kinds of wine produced in the Rheingau, the domination of the *Riesling* grape variety means they tend to be elegant and positive among German wines with the fragrant *Riesling* bouquet a striking characteristic.

RHEINHESSEN

The principal grape variety of Rheinhessen is the *Sylvaner* which produces light, pleasant wines which are drunk young and which generally lack the distinction of the wine from *Riesling* grapes.

Perhaps the region's most important claim to fame among wine enthusiasts is that it is the home of *Liebfraumilch* which has become a general term for light, pleasant but undemanding German wines but which once referred specifically to the vineyards below the Liebfrauenkirche church in the town of Reims.

Rheinhessen runs along the Rhine between Worms and Bingen and is the largest wine growing area in Germany but the second in production. Wine has a long history here; viticulture was practised at least as early as the 13th century.

Apart from the *Sylvaner* grape which produces the characteristically soft *Liebfraumilch* style, there are other grape varieties — *Riesling* in the south, *Müller-Thurgau* (now the most widely planted grape in Germany); *Scheurebe*, *Kerner* and *Farrebe*, as well as red grapes.

Some of the vineyards producing the finest *Rheinhessen* wines are at Nierstein, Nackenheim and Dipenheim.

The Goldene Luft vineyard in Nierstein *(right)*.

RHEINPFALZ
OR PALATINATE

Rheinpfalz or Palatinate, as it is known in English, is a rich, fertile region in which just about everything seems to grow: cherries, peaches, figs, almonds and, of course, vines.

Bordered by Rheinhessen in the north and France to the south and west, the region produces more wine than any other in Germany.

It is a beguiling landscape of tiny villages with half-timbered houses and inviting inns where the local wine and food can be sampled. In the days of Charlemagne it was known as the 'wine cellar of the Holy Roman Empire' and now provides wines for discriminating palates at home and abroad. An ancient highway, said to be some 2000 years old, the *Weinstrasse* (wine road) winds through the villages and vineyards.

The best wine comes from the northern half of the region; classic *Riesling* comes from Wackenheim, Bad Durkheim and Deidesheim and gentle, flowery wines from the *Müller-Thurgau* grape variety is also produced in the favoured soil which has special attributes. This soil, with the climate, gives the Palatinate the headiest, heaviest wines of Germany. Wine of *Kabinett* and *Spätlese* categories is regularly produced and, in years when conditions are right, the exquisite *Trockenbeerenauslese*, especially from the Von Buhl vineyards at Deidesheim and the Burklin-Wolf estates at Wachenheim.

Traditional vine harvesting equipment *(below)*.

This machine *(right)* is used for trimming the tops of the vines.

In the southern half of the region, the wines do not usually achieve such a high degree of quality and most wine is drunk young. A local favourite, which is not seen outside the area, is a very young, cloudy wine called *Federweisser* (feather white).

MOSEL - SAAR - RUWER

Mosel and Rhine wines can easily be distinguished because Rhine wine is bottled in brown bottles and Mosel in green bottles. The green colour is appropriate for the wines of Mosel, suggesting their young, fresh, Spring-like qualities.

It is an ancient wine growing area. Archaeological evidence supports the claim that wine has been produced in this green, hilly country for some 2000 years. Trier, where the Mosel becomes a German river, is an ancient Roman city, and it runs from here to the Rhine at Koblenz, running through beautiful valleys with incredibly steep hills where the vines grow high on terraces on the hillsides which are sometimes so steep that they can be reached only by ladders.

The best wines come from the middle of the Mosel, from the *Riesling* grape which was the exclusive grape of the region in 1787 by order of the Elector of Trier. The slatey soil gives the best Mosel *Rieslings* a distinctive character, sometimes a flinty

Recently harvested grapes *(above)*.

This splendid view from the Doktor vineyard shows the town of Bernkastel and the adjacent bridge *(left)*.

flavour. Most Mosel wines are drunk young and are appreciated for their flowery freshness but some achieve mature elegance. Classic wines of this type come from the villages of Piesport, Trittenheim, Neumagen, Dhron, Braunberg, Bernkastel and some of the most famous vineyards in Germany are Bernkastel Döktor and Wehlener Sonnenhuhe.

More *Riesling* is grown in the Mosel region than anywhere else in Germany but it is no longer the exclusive grape variety. *Müller-Thurgau* is widely planted in the upper and lower Mosel and produces light, pleasing wines of mild character.

The other wine growing regions grow wine from approved grape varieties produce wine with individual character — Baden in the Black Forest, produces fragrant, spicy, aromatic white wines which have a pronounced powerful style; the robust wines of Franken, the most easterly of Germany's wine growing regions are bottled in traditional green flagons; Nahe wines from the Nahe river region are fruity, full of flavour; the castle country of Mittelrhein produces white wines which are fresh, sharper, more austere than wine from other regions. Ahr, the most northern wine growing region, is known for fresh, lively white wines and Hessiche Bergstrasse, the smallest wine growing region of Germany, has a reputation for hearty wines with more body than is sometimes the case.

RED WINES OF GERMANY

Germany's international reputation as a wine country is based on its range of quality white wines but red wine is produced, although rarely seen outside Germany. As a rule, the red wine is fruitier, lighter, with less tannin than the red wine of France.

The three red grape varieties are *Spätburgunder* (the *Pinot Noir* of Burgundy originally) which produces a fairly full bodied wine and *Portugieser* and *Trollinger* which produce light, refreshing reds.

SPAIN

Spain has more land devoted to the growing of wines than any other European country, although it is not the largest producer, coming behind Italy and France. However, it is an important wine country, not only because of the volume of wine it produces but because of the quality of its best wines.

It is a country with a bright wine future and poses a threat to the dominance of France and, more particularly, Italy in the years ahead, especially when it is a full member of the European Economic Community. Standards have improved greatly over recent years with more wines qualifying for the *Denominación de Origen* which sets standards governing the production of wines in defined areas and is similar to the French *Appellation Controlée*.

Sulphuring the barrel *(above)* is always necessary to ensure that the barrel is totally disinfected before the new wine is inserted.

——— RED WINES ——— OF SPAIN

The best red wine comes from the north of the country, from the ancient kingdom of Navarre, in the wine district of Rioja, in the valley of the Ebro river. The name of the district comes from a tributary of the Ebro, the Río Oja.

The district is divided into two parts: the Río Alta or high Rioja, and the Río Baja, the low Rioja. The best reds are found the in temperate climate of the Rioja Alta; the wines of the warmer, drier Rioja Baja tend to be heavier and coarser.

Wine has been produced in Rioja since the Middle Ages but a major influence came from Bordeaux in the last century when French wine growers came to the region, escaping from the dreaded phylloxera — the tiny beetle-like creature from North America which attacked the roots of the vines and swept through the vineyards of Europe in the 19th century — which had devastated their vineyards. The infusion of Bordeaux wine growing methods led to an improvement of local methods but the wines of Bordeaux and Rioja are quite different, even though some attempts have been made to liken the lighter wines of Rioja to the clarets of Bordeaux.

The best Rioja is light in character; deep in colour; full in taste and with a distinctive oaky flavour which comes from long storage in oak casks.

Although vineyards are sometimes given on labels, they are used as brand names rather than as precise indications of where the wine originated. Among the best of these — given with unhesitating confidence by any Spanish wine waiter — are *Marqués de Riscal* and *Marqués de Murrieta*.

The wines are often described as '*clarete*' which is a light red and '*tinto*' which is more full bodied. *Reserva* on the label indicates a wine from good vintage years, well aged — although all *Riojas* are kept in cask for four to five years.

For many people, *Rioja* is the first and last word on Spanish wine but there are others which are well worth attention, although they are not seen outside Spain as much as the wines of

A familiar sight *(below)*, vines bathed
in a morning mist.

A typical Spanish vineyard *(right)*.
When the vines are in leaf they make
a vivid contrast to the albariza soil.

Rioja. There are excellent reds from the Penades district of
Catalonia, a region which produces as great a variety of wines as
any in Spain.

Wines from the Navarra are made from the same grape
varieties and in the same way as those of Rioja and are almost
identical.

Valladolid produces a number of red wines worth seeking out
and the neighbouring *Vega Sicilia*, made from a blend of French
grapes, matured for long periods in oak, is a remarkable wine: full,
complex, with a high alcohol level of 13.5 per cent. It is also rare
as production is limited.

The plains of La Mancha in central Spain produce a vast
amount of wine, much of which goes into blended wines, but
Valdapenas is a pleasing wine in its own right.

WHITE WINES OF SPAIN

Spain produces a considerable quantity of white wine but most of
it is pleasant rather than distinguished as the climate is not ideal
for the production of white wine.

Rioja white wines are among the best available. They have a
quite individual style as the wine is stored for longer than is usual
with white wines, which gives an unusual richness and flavour.

The Penades district is best known for its sparkling white wine,
made in the *méthode champenoise*, and very good in its own way
but not like French *champagne*. There are some crisp, dry still
white wines from this district and popular dry Catalan white wines
from Alella. Most of the white wine is found in the north as the
climate in the south is too fierce for anything but the sturdiest red.

SHERRY

Sherry is Spain's great gift to the world of wine. Perhaps the most familiar of all wines, the most civilized, the most acceptable of all aperitifs.

There are, of course, wines from other countries which are described as sherry, some of which are pleasant enough. But there is only one true sherry and that comes from the deep south of Spain, in Andalusia where Nature and man come together to create this unique wine. Andalusia is the essential Spain; a region of flamenco and bulls and steely pride. The centre of the sherry region is Jerez de la Frontera; the word 'sherry' is a corruption of the name, the result of English attempts to grapple with the fruity, chewy language of Andalusia.

The English have always been partial to sherry: Sir Francis

Tilling the soil between the rows of vines *(left)*.

In the sherry nurseries, the progress of every cask is checked at least once a year. To do this the bodega master uses a *venecia*, a silver cup with a long, thin whalebone handle *(left)*. He dips the rod deep into the cask, to penetrate the *flor*, then withdraws his sample and whips it around his head to clear it before pouring it out.

Drake carried off butts of it after sacking Cadiz; Shakespeare had Falstaff sing its praises — it was called sack at that time. He said, after praising its excellent effect on his wit: 'If I had a thousand sons, the first human principle I would teach them should be to forswear thin potations, and to addict themselves to sack.'

The sherry grape is the *Palomino*, a green and golden grape, the colour of sherry itself. The best vineyards are on chalky soil, as in other countries. The making of sherry is an involved and mysterious process. The ripe grapes, high in sugar content from months of exposure to the sun, are given an even higher sugar level by being spread out on mats of esparto grass and dried.

The grapes are usually pressed by mechanical means these days but in some places the traditional method is followed in which men wearing special boots tread the grapes in the cool of the night. Fermentation follows quickly; a fierce, violent eruption as the yeast begins to work. The real life of the wine begins in the cathedrals of Jerez — the bodegas, vast sheds where the wine undergoes the long transition from innocent, youthful wine to subtle mature sherry.

When the young wine has fermented and been fortified by the addition of brandy — after about two years usually — it is introduced into the blending process or 'solerna' system. This is a series of barrels containing wines of different ages and at different stages of development. The new wine is placed in the top row of

Palomino is the sherry grape. Green and golden in colour, it flourishes on chalky soil *(left)*.

casks and will move down the rows over the years to the bottom level of casks from which the wine is drawn.

As the wine leaves the cask, it is replenished from the level above which, in turn, is replenished by wine from the next upper level and so on. There are many different groups of solernas in the bodega for different kinds of sherry — *fino*, *amontillado*, etc. The progress of the wine through the system may take from four to 12 years.

There is much that is mysterious in the making of sherry. The way the new and old wines blend is subtle and complex; the new wine merging into a corporate identity with the passage of time. But the most remarkable part of the process is the '*flor*', a white yeast, which appears on some casks and gives the special, highly prized quality of sherry to the wine, creating the best *finos*. The flor does not appear on all casks and it is not known why it appears or fails to appear. It simply is part of the mystery of sherry.

The main types of sherry are:

Fino. Sherry from the bodegas of Jerez de la Frontera. Dry, light, delicate but can age well.

Amontillado. Older than a *fino*. Dry but with a fullness of taste. Cheaper versions can be disappointingly sweet.

Manzanilla. Very light, dry with a flowery scent, from the bodegas of Anlucar de Barrameda on the coast.

Oloroso. Dark, full sherry, not affected by the *flor*. Dry but can be made into a sweet, dessert wine by the addition of wine from the Pedro Ximenes grape variety.

Outside the recognized sherry area, east of Seville, is the wine district of Montilla which produces a wine of great character and strength that is practically indistinguishable from sherry.

It is extremely popular in Spain, especially as an aperitif. The grape variety here is *Pedro Ximenes* rather than *Palomino*, which produces wine of such enormous natural strength in the great heat of the region — about 16 per cent — that there is no need for an addition of brandy. The wine is as Nature intended and mankind hoped.

A beautiful bodega *(below)*
where the real life of the wine begins.

HARVEY'S PORTS

THE DIRECTOR'S BIN
VERY SUPERIOR OLD TAWNY DRY

JOHN HARVEY & SONS, Ltd.
BRISTOL, Eng.

FOUNDED 1796

OTHER COUNTRIES

In the spring, the young port is shipped off to the lodges at the mouth of the river opposite Oporto *(above)*.

Portugal is fourth in the league of European wine producing countries; behind Italy, France and Spain, but ahead of Germany. The country is often thought of only in terms of the two wine extremes, port and rosé, but it has a variety of wines, many of which are underrated.

Port was an English invention in the 18th century, born of that fertile parent of invention, necessity. Wine from France was barred from English tables during the Napoleonic wars and new sources of supply were sought. Portuguese wine was plentiful and available but too strong for English tastes. However, it was discovered that the addition of brandy during fermentation would prevent the wine from achieving too high a level of alcohol and preserve the desired level of sweetness.

The English loved it; especially the upper classes for whom several bottles at a sitting was regarded as modest. Now the taste is shared by other social groups, although the consumption at a sitting has been considerably reduced, and many more countries — the French, for example — have developed a considerable partiality for port.

The vineyards where the grapes for port are grown are in the bleak, mountainous country of the upper Douro where the fierce, unyielding sun causes the grapes to grow thick black skins and it is the colour from these that gives port its superb, luxurious colour that is an integral part of its attraction.

Mechanical methods have been introduced for pressing, replacing the ancient method where large groups of older men and boys trod the grapes in bare feet in the late evening, singing traditional songs as they moved backwards and forwards over the purple mush. Treading the grapes with bare feet pressed the colour out of the skins without crushing the pips and stalks which would leave a taste in the wine.

The young wine, with its addition of brandy, is stored in cellars until the spring when it is shipped off to school, to the great lodges — equivalent to the bodegas of Jerez — at the mouth of the river, opposite Oporto. The influence of the English, the creators of port, is still strong and is expressed in the names of the great shippers, such as Croft, Cockburn and Taylor.

The essential ingredient of port is age. Time is necessary to make the transition from simple wine with added brandy to the powerful, smooth, complex character of port. As with sherry, blending is the crucial stage. The wine is usually made from a blend of various grapes from different vineyards and years. The exception is vintage port which is made from wine of a particular year and not mixed with other wines. A vintage year is one which the shippers believe to be outstandingly good. Such years are declared somewhat infrequently, perhaps once every three or four years.

Vintage port is bottled after two years in wood and does its

Port being aged and matured in wooden casks *(right)*.

ageing in bottle, a process which may take from twenty to forty years. This long-maturing wine is usually bought for laying down for future enjoyment, perhaps by future generations. During the ageing a deposit develops in the bottle and the wine has to be carefully decanted to avoid the deposit or crust mixing with the wine.

Late bottled vintage port is matured in wood for about five or six years and bottled after the deposit has formed and been left in the wooden cask.

Tawny port is matured in wooden casks; the best is stored for up to 15 years. In time, it arrives at a beautiful tawny colour and is bottled when it is ready to drink. Ruby port is also aged in wood but is bottled earlier, when the colour is still a deep ruby red. White port is made from white grapes and is available sweet or dry. There is no vintage white port.

The red wines of Dao, from the centre of Portugal are becoming widely known and appreciated. The finest are smooth,

Harvesting the vines is much the same in Portugal as it is elsewhere *(left)*.

velvety, but with considerable character. They usually age in wood for up to three years and can continue developing in the bottle for up to 12 years. *Reserva* on the label indicates the wine has been aged for even longer than usual, which means it will have greater fulness and a longer bottle life.

Colares is another fine red, said to be the best in Portugal by some enthusiasts. Grown in sand, which usually produces good wine, the wine is high in tannin and needs a long period of maturing.

Apart from port, Portugal is probably best known for the sweet slightly sparkling rosé which is dismissed by experts but which continues to be enjoyed by many. More interesting is the '*vinho verde*', the 'green wines' of Portugal. They are fresh, slightly sparkling with an edge of acidity. White wines of Dao are big and dry and there is an outstanding sweet dessert wine, *Moscatel de Setubal* from near Lisbon.

Madeira is a fortified wine, a relation of port, although it has a

Traditionally, the young port was taken downstream to shippers at Vila Nova de Gaia, near Oporto, in fat *barco rabelos (above)*, boats which could carry up to 60 pipes at a time.

distinct and individual character.

The Portuguese island of Madeira in the Atlantic was once a stopping point for ships bound for the Cape of Good Hope and India. The origins of *Madeira* wine come from this time when it was discovered that the simple red wine of the island changed character on its journey across the equator, becoming rich and smooth with a deep, red brown colour.

The long sea voyage through increasing temperatures is copied in the method which is used to make *Madeira* wine. The wine is heated for a period of six weeks up to 50 degrees Centigrade and allowed to cool for the same period. The method sounds barbaric but it produces wine of great power and longevity — there are many examples of *Madeira* happily surviving more than 100 years old.

The main types are:
Sercial: light, dry and fragrant
Malmsey: very sweet, dark brown, beautiful dessert wine
Bual: sweet but light, the most well known *Madeira*
Verdelho: semi sweet but light in style.

AUSTRIA

Austria is white wine country, producing pleasing light table wines and distinguished, golden wine. The best is probably from the beautiful district of Wachau on the Danube. Here, light gold, fragrant wine is made from the Rhine *Riesling* grape variety and fuller whites from the Austrian *Grüner Vetliner* variety. *Sylvaner* is also grown and used for fresh, fruity and generally cheaper wine.

In and around Vienna the vineyards produce an abundance of cheerful wine from a number of grape varieties, including the *Grüner Vetliner* and *Traminer*. In the wine villages, the locals drink *Heurige*, new wine straight from the cask in enormous quantities, accompanied by plenty of food and — for this is Vienna — music.

The charmingly-named Gumpoldskirchen is the centre of Austria's leading wine regions and produces what many regard as the country's finest achievement in wine: golden, sweet, of great fragrance.

The ancient town of Rust on the border with Hungary produces some heady wines, the most remarkable of which are made from grapes with the *Botrytis Cinerea* or noble rot. From these shrivelled grapes, high in sugar content, comes the heavy, golden, honey-sweet *Trockenbeerenauslese*.

A typical Austrian vineyard *(below)* set in the foothills of the Alps.

Bull's Blood *(right)*, a wine noted among other things for the depth of its colour.

—— *HUNGARY* ——

Hungary has a long and noble tradition of wine making. In the 9th century AD, the Magyars rode out of the Asiatic steppes and settled on the great plains of what is now Hungary. They knew the art of wine-making and developed the vineyards they found which had been established by the Romans.

The most famous wine of Hungary is the legendary *Tokay*, a golden, sweet but powerful wine with a marvellous bouquet. The finest *Tokay* is made from grapes with the 'noble rot' of *Sauternes* or the 'aszu' of Hungary.

There are several types of *Tokay*, all protected by quality controls, including the most common, *Furmint*; *Tokay Szamarodni*, made from normally ripe and overripe grapes and the noblest of them all, *Tokay Aszu*, favoured by monarchs from Louis XIV to Peter the Great.

The powerful red wine from Eger in the north east of Hungary

It is often necessary to protect the vines from bird attacks by covering them with netting *(above)*.

The golden yellow Szurkebarat *(above)* flourishes in the area north of Lake Balaton.

is better known as *Bull's Blood*, a romantic name but one which reflects something of the character of the wine. According to legend, the deep colour of the wine was achieved by the addition of bulls' blood but the more prosaic truth is that the colour comes from the different red grapes used. The name is also said to come from the 16th century, when Eger was invaded by the Turks. The locals are said to have fortified themselves for battle with liberal helpings of their favourite wine and their valour was such that the Turks believed that their ferocious opponents had 'drunk the blood of bulls'.

Of Hungary's 14 wine-growing regions, the most attractive must surely be the area north of Lake Balaton, the largest stretch of inland water in Europe, known as the Hungarian Sea. The climate is sunny and warm and the soil of basalt (which absorbs the heat), clay and sand is ideal for vines.

The golden yellow *Szurkebarat*, known as *Pinot Gris* in France, flourishes here producing smooth but powerful white

A vineyard devoted to the Olasz Riesling grape *(above)*.

wines. The most prolific grape of the area is *Olasz Riesling* which provides most of the area's wine.

Ketnyelu produces a fine, dry, green-gold wine. It is the oldest grape variety of the region and its name means 'blue stalk' after the blue of the leaf stalk.

The small district of Somlo produces a wine of great reputation. Requiring long periods of maturing to achieve its potential, the wine is said to have therapeutic qualities and was traditionally prescribed for the male Hapsburg royalty before their wedding nights to ensure the succession of a male heir.

In the north, the aptly-named *Mor* grape produces a full, heavy white wine with an alcohol content of 12-13 per cent.

SWITZERLAND

The Swiss, known for their practical approach to life, take an appropriately sensible attitude towards the wine they produce: they drink most of it themselves.

The white wines are the best, especially the dry light wines from around Lake Neuchatel which is also made into sparkling wine by the *méthode champenoise*. *Fendant* is a light, refreshing white wine made from the *Chasselas* grape.

Good red wines come from the Ticino, in the Italian-speaking region in the south, and the Dole area where the red wine is a blend of *Gamay* and *Pinot Noir* varieties.

LUXEMBOURG

This tiny country produces only white wines from vineyards along the steep banks of the Moselle. The principal grape varieties are *Riesling*, *Rivaner* (or *Müller-Thurgau* as it is known elswhere) and *Traminer*. Luxembourg *Moselles* tend to be even lighter than their German counterparts and not as fine, but they have a fresh, fragrant delicacy that is admired.

YUGOSLAVIA

The *Riesling* grape variety is widely planted in the north of Yugoslavia and produces a white medium-dry wine which is exported in considerable quantities.

This grape variety is the *Laski Riesling* which produces a wine similar to that of the Rhine variety but is a little stronger. Other white grape varieties in the northern province of Slovania are *Sylvaner* and *Traminer*, producing similar, fresh, agreeable but not outstanding wines. The wines are usually known by the grape variety from which they are made with extra identification coming with the name of the district — for example, *Lutomer*,

An extensive collection of baskets
(below) for harvesting the vines.

Pruning young vines *(above)* near the beautiful village of Mostar.

which is the best known town of the northern region, precedes the grape variety, *Riesling*, on the label.

An unexpected wine in this region of dry medium white wines is a heavy, sweet white wine made from late-picked grapes with the somewhat alarming name of *Tiger's Milk* or *Tigrio Kleko*, presumably because of its tigerish qualities.

The celebrated *Zilavka*, from the ancient and beautiful town of Mostar, is a grand wine: dry but full bodied and high in alcohol.

The red wines are from the south and *Prokupac* from Serbia is one of the best known; a robust wine which can have a strong fruitiness.

Merlot and *Cabernet Sauvignon* are grown on the Dalmatian coast and produce big, full wines.

The colour and strength of the wine increases further down the coast: *Faros*, a ruby-red wine from the *Plavac Mali* grape has an alcohol content of more than 13 per cent. Even greater in alcoholic strength is *Proshek*, a sweet dessert wine made from grapes which have been dried in the sun which has 15 per cent alcohol.

GREECE

Among the many debts the world at large owes to Greece is one of gratitude for the gift of wine. Greece was the original home of wine and it was Greeks who took the good news to Rome and spread the word throughout the Mediterranean.

Times have changed but tastes have remained remarkably faithful in Greece where resinated wines are as popular today as they were 2500 years ago. Non-Greeks do not always share the enthusiasm for this dry white wine, low in alcohol, to which pine resin — originally a preservative — is now added to provide flavour.

Unresinated wines are appearing though — for example *Agiorgitko*, a dry, full bodied red from Corinth and *Domestica* light reds and dry whites.

Grape pickers are renowned for the huge appetites produced by the long hours and physically demanding work. Estates cater for this by providing a substantial meal for all the pickers *(left)*.

BULGARIA

Bulgaria's wine story is remarkable. It can claim an antiquity greater than any other European country as some myths have it that the Greek wine god, Dionysus, came from the Rhodope mountains.

But viticulture was not a major preoccupation of the Moslem Turks who ruled the country from the 14th to the 19th centuries. It was after World War II that the government set about improving, indeed transforming, the wine industry.

Their success has been extraordinary. In a few years, Bulgaria shot up the league of wine-producing countries and now exports three-quarters of its wine to 70 countries.

This success can be explained by the use of the latest wine-processing equipment and technology and the use of proven, classic grape varieties such as the *Riesling* and *Cabernet Sauvignon* — the latter is really at home in Bulgaria, producing an excellent wine which displays considerable depth and robustness.

These grapes are being put into the hopper *(right)* by a rotating fork-lift truck.

ENGLAND

England is much more a consumer of wine than a producer but it does have a small wine industry producing wines of quality rather than quantity for consumption on the home market.

The establishing of an indigenous wine industry has finally been achieved which must be satisfying for the pioneers who were assured it was impossible in England. Vines were grown in Roman times and a number of vineyards are recorded in Domesday, but it was generally felt that wine production was not feasible in modern times.

The modern wine industry is concentrated in the southern half of England: in Essex, Hampshire, but mainly in the Kent and Sussex Weald at places like Lamberhurst in Kent (where the vineyards can be seen on the hillside on the road through the village), Biddenden, Penshurst and Horam. The main grape varieties are *Müller-Thurgau* and *Sylval Blanc* and the wine produced is German in style — light, fragrant, delicate.

Supervising the fermentation process in stainless steel vats *(left)*.

TASTING

Wine tasting has become associated with wine snobbery in the minds of some people; a ritual where supercilious bores exchange references such as 'the south side of the hill' and 'an amusing but not boorish wine' and other displays of dubious expertise.

All of which is a pity because wine tasting is the best way of understanding more about wine. Like any other subject, knowledge of wine is acquired by study and experience. A painting or a piece of music must be examined, re-examined, considered in a number of ways, if it is to be fully appreciated. So it is with wine.

The purpose of wine tasting is much more than to establish if the wine is good or bad, as experienced tasters can discover fine nuances of character when examining a wine.

There is, of course, a world of difference between the professional taster and the amateur. The professional tastes for practical reasons: to discover the development of the wine during its life; to decide on the commercial value of the wine before purchasing; to test for an official level of quality.

The 'smell' of the wine is — some people claim — the most significant indicator to its quality. Great care should be taken when tasting to ensure that the bouquet is released *(above)*.

The professional tester is necessarily critical, seeking to discover the shortcomings of the wine. The amateur is more concerned with finding out about the virtues of the wine, and, indeed, in drinking some of it.

Despite these different approaches, the method of tasting is the same. The faculties of sight, smell and taste are used — in that order. The colour of wine is a sensuous experience in itself; from the mysterious depths of a *St Emilion* to the clear, shining red of a young *Beaujolais* or the golden tints of *Sancerre* to the green echoes of *Chablis*.

The colour also provides information about the quality and age of the wine. White wines grow darker with age; red wines grow lighter, the youthful red deepening into purple and brown. As the wine ages, it is possible to detect a pale border at the edge.

The sense of smell may play the greatest part in the tasting of wine. Indeed, it has been claimed that smell and taste are a single composite sense and it is true that it is impossible to taste when one cannot use the sense of smell, when one has a cold, for example.

The glass should be rotated slowly to allow the oxygen to reach the wine and stimulate the release of the bouquet. The aroma produces almost endless associations and ideas in different wines: the tang of the sea in *Muscadet*; the smoky suggestion of *Montrachet*; the distinctive fruit-filled scent of *Beaujolais*; the surprisingly powerful flowery bouquet of a delicate *Moselle*.

These smells trigger the memory, identifying the wine and, very often, the circumstances in which they were first encountered — encouraging more remembrances of times enjoyed.

Finally, there is the taste, the sensation of the wine in the mouth. A reasonable mouthful should be taken, rather than a reverential sip, which should be rolled around the mouth,

This sample tap on the fermentation vat *(right)* is used for taking samples for analysis and tasting during fermentation.

When taking a sample from a cask which is on ¾-bung *(left)*, a wooden pin is removed and the flow of the wine from the hole is caused by exerting pressure on the cask head using the hammer as a lever.

forwards, backwards and from side to side, as if chewing. It is at this point that the character of the wine is fully revealed: the promise of colour and bouquet combining with the powerful, spicy richness of a good red from the Côtes du Rhône or the light, refreshing charm of a quality white wine from the Loire.

Professional wine tasters spit out the wine after tasting, which is a sensible idea when many wines are tasted. Some say that amateurs should do the same but most amateurs disagree and most amateur wine tastings are social occasions rather than sober business meetings.

The usual rules for the order of tasting are: dry wines before medium dry or sweet; young before old; modest before fine; white before red; light before heavy.

The ideal tasting glass is the conventional tulip shape which should be of clear glass so the colour of the wine can be seen. The glass should be two-thirds full so the taster can inhale the bouquet, not full to the brim, which could lead to the taster inhaling the wine.

There is an extensive vocabulary of wine used by wine tasters; a common language in which fairly imprecise terms have accepted meanings. It is worth knowing some of these, although it is likely that one's own discoveries and descriptions will seem more apt and striking.

A few of these terms are:

ACIDITY: can be a virtue or a vice. It can provide a satisfyingly crisp bite or it might be too tart and harsh. Lack of acidity can led to soft, flat, uninteresting sweetish wine.

AGREEABLE: a well balanced wine, pleasant to drink.

HEADY: wine with a high level of alcohol.

ROBUST: a full bodied wine.

QUAFFING: used to describe a wine that is easy to drink, rather than one that should be treated with the greatest respect.

LIGHT: a wine light in alcohol.

SWEET: the description can cover a range of sweetness, from

This cartoon hanging in the cellar at Château Pétrus *(above)* depicts a *maître de chais* holding a *tastevin*.

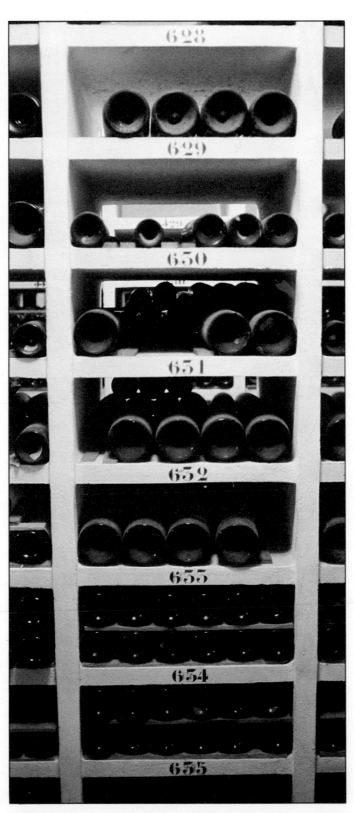

Numbered bins *(right)* are used for storing old wines.

Tasting takes place at many stages of
the wine-making process. Here
(below) a young wine is being tasted
straight from the barrel.

barely escaping dry to heavy, syrupy sweetness.

BALANCED: a wine in which all the elements are in proportion, without excessive characteristics.

ROUND: a balanced wine, smooth and full bodied.

DRY: a wine with no residual sugar, fully fermented.

SUPPLE: easy to drink and taste with little or no evidence of tannin.

VELVETY: a mellow wine, soft as velvet.

GREEN: young, unbalanced wine with too much acidity.

FINESSE: distinction, delicacy, particularly of bouquet.

One of the most mis-used wine terms is 'corked' which is often used to describe wine in which tiny pieces of cork may have dropped when the bottle was opened, and is usually accompanied by the belief that the wine is somehow contaminated.

The cork does not damage the wine in any way and the cork should simply be removed. There is no difficulty in recognizing genuinely corked wine and it has a distinctly unpleasant smell and taste. The condition is caused by faulty corks which allow oxygen to make contact with the wine.

Temperature is another aspect of wine which appears to cause confusion and uncertainty. Light red wines shoud be served at fairly cool temperature of 10 and 12 degrees Centigrade, but fuller red wines should be served at the temperature of a fairly warm room — between 16 and 18 degrees Centigrade.

White and rosé wines should be served cool, at between 8 and 12 degrees Centigrade but should not be too cold that the taste is affected. Sweet white wines, *champagne* and sparkling wines should be served cool, between 6 and 8 degrees Centigrade.

STORING WINE

The great days of cellars stocked with rows of documented wines have largely disappeared, along with venerable butlers and visiting wine merchants.

But it is still worthwhile creating a small area for the storage of wine, not only to have a stock of wines to hand but to store wines which need time to mature.

The wine store should be fairly cool, from 10 to 14 degrees Centigrade, as too much heat will age wine prematurely. It should also be dark as too much light will affect the wine — neon lighting must be avoided. Quiet is desirable as vibrations from traffic or passageways can have a detrimental effect on the wine.

MONTALCINO
ORIGINE CONTROLLATA
I-SANTI
PROPRIA
LLA FATTORIA "IL GREPPO "
RANCO Biondi Santi *viticultore nella*
ENDA Agricola"Greppo"
MONTALCINO·ITALIA   0,750 litri

CHINON
APPELLATION CHINON CONTRÔLÉE
MIS EN BOUTEILLE A LA PROPRIÉTÉ   75d

ABEL DUMONT, PROPRIÉTAIRE-VITICULTEUR A 37500 CRAVANT-LES-COTEAUX

Deinhard   KOBLENZ · GERMANY
AN RHEIN & MOSEL
LED BY
D & CO.   A. P. Nr. 590700300782
of Germany   1794
G. E G R.
HANNS CHRISTOF
Kabinett
Qualitätswein mit Prädikat
Bereich
Südliche Weinstraße
Rheinpfalz
0 ml

MOSEL · SAAR · RUWER
19   81
BERNKASTELER DOKTOR
RIESLING SPÄTLESE
QUALITÄTSWEIN MIT PRÄDIKAT · A. P. Nr. 157628102182
Erzeugerabfüllung · Estate bottled · Gutsverwaltung
Deinhard
Bernkastel-Kues/Koblenz

SHIPPED BY
Deinhard &Co   REGISTERED TRA
KOBLENZ · GERMANY
750 ml
PRODUCE OF GERMANY   75

FONDÉE   EN 1860
BEAUNE 1er CRU
CENT VIGNES
APPELLATION BEAUNE 1er CRU CONTRÔLÉE
Prosper Maufoux   750 ml
MIS EN BOUTEILLES PAR MAISON PROSPER MAUFOUX
NÉGOCIANT A SANTENAY (COTE-D'OR) - FRANCE
PRODUCE OF FRANCE   TD. LONDON

CHIANTI
CLASSICO
DENOMINAZIONE DI ORIGINE CONTROLLATA
RODANO
Imbottigliato dal viticolto
TTORIO POZZESI
ITALIA

MEURSAULT
APPELLATION MEURSAULT CONTROLÉE

Prosper Maufoux

750 ml

MIS EN BOUTEILLES PAR MAISON PROSPER MAUFOUX
NÉGOCIANT À SANTENAY (COTE-D'OR) - FRANCE
PRODUCE OF FRANCE

SOLE IMPORTERS DEINHARD & CO. LTD. LONDON

FRASCATI
DENOMINAZIONE DI ORIGINE CONTROLLATA

IMBOTTIGLIATO DALLA
CANTINA SOCIALE COOPERATIVA DI MARINO
NELLE PROPRIE CANTINE DI FRATTOCCHIE DI MARINO (ROMA) ITALIA

11.5 % VOL.

750 ml. ℮   cod. imb.1217 Roma

R.I. 247/Roma

Frascati
Superiore
denominazione di origine controllata
imbottigliato nelle cantine
Pavan
Lariano-Italia

0,700 litri   12% vol.

FATTORIA MONTELLORI
CHIANTI
Denominazione di origine controllata

Vigneti in Cerreto Guidi
Prop. Giuseppe Nieri imbottigliate
Fucecchio - Italia

R.I. 584 / FI

0.750 LT.

Deinhard
KOBLENZ · GERMANY
AN RHEIN & MOSEL

BOTTLED BY
DEINHARD & CO.

DEINMOSELLE

Mosel · Saar · Ruwer
Qualitätswein · A.P. Nr. 190700300882

GERMANY

AG

BAROLO
DENOMINAZIONE DI ORIGINE CONTROL
V.Q.P.R.D.

VINIFICATO E IMBOTTIGLIATO IN ZONA DI
ASCHERI GIACOM

BRA - VIA G. PIUMATI 19

GLOSSARY

Small capitals indicate cross references.

Foreign words are indicated by the letters *Fr* (French), *Ger* (German) and *It* (Italian) after the headword.

Acetic acid Traces of acetic acid are present in all wines, but usually in amounts too small to be detected by taste or smell. Sometimes, usually as a result of bad handling, the acetobacter microbe attacks the wine causing it to acetify and giving it the vinegary taste and smell characteristic of sour or spoiled wine. Acetic acid is a volatile acid.

Acidity There are several kinds of acid present in wines. These acids are important. Not only do they help the wine keep well, they also give it an edge without which it would taste flat. There are three kinds of acidity involved in the winemaking process: volatile, fixed and total acidity. Volatile acidity includes acids such as acetic acid which are not present in the fresh grape juice but are produced during vinification; fixed acidity included the natural fruit acids — tartaric, malic and citric acid; together volatile acidity and fixed acidity make up total acidity.

Alcohol The sugar in grapes is converted by yeasts into ethyl alcohol (C_2H_6O) and carbon dioxide gas—the process is called ALCOHOLIC FERMENTATION. Alcohol is a colourless, volatile liquid which is toxic. Taken in small quantities it has a pleasing and soporific effect.

Alcoholic content Methods of measuring the alcoholic strength of wines and spirits vary from country to country. A percentage per volume scale is now generally used in Europe.

Anthocyanines These are chemicals which result from the breakdown of the tannin and colouring substances in wine. They sometimes cause haze and deposits which must be stabilized by coagulation and precipitation with FINING AGENTS such as gelatin, egg whites etc.

Appellation Contrôlée (AC) *(Fr)* The highest rank in the APPELLATION D'ORIGINE system. These two words on a label guarantee the origin and production standards of the wine.

Appellation d'Origine Contrôlée (AOC) *(Fr)* This is a classification of French wine which is regulated by a body known as the Institut National des Appellations d'Origine des Vins et Eaux-de-Vie (INAO) which was set up in 1935. This organization dictates not only the name which a wine carries, but also regulates very strictly the viticulture and vinification procedures: type of grape; degree of ripeness when picked and so on. The Appellation Contrôlée wines are the most strictly controlled. The second category are the Vins Délimités de Qualité Supérieure (VDQS) wines. Both AOC and VDQS wines are VQPRD or Vins de Qualité Produits dans une Région Déterminée, following these are the Vins de Pays and lastly the Vins de Table.

Aroma The aroma of a wine is that part of its smell which is derived from the grape and should be distinguished from the bouquet which develops in the bottle. It is most pronounced when the wine is young. Certain varieties of grape such as the Muscat are easily identified by their smell, although much of this disappears during the fermentation process. Aroma tends to fade as the wine is aged and in good wines the bouquet should take over.

Assemblage *(Fr)* A term which describes the blending of wines of different origin, characteristics or age. Fine wines are not usually blended, but wines from different casks may be 'assembled' to avoid cask-to-cask differences. The vin de press and the vin de goutte of a particular vineyard are often blended.

Auslese *(Ger)* the third of the German QUALITÄTSWEIN MIT PRÄDIKAT wines—the categories above it are Beerenauslese and Trockenbeerenauslese. Auslese grapes are picked late in the harvest when they will be ripest. Only the very ripest bunches are selected so Auslese wines will be sweeter and more expensive than the Spätlese from the same cellar and the same vintage. It must by law have an Oechsle reading of 97°.

Balling Hydrometer scale used in America to measure the approximate sugar content of unfermented grape juice—from this the probable alcohol content of the finished wine can be calculated.

Barrel The containers in which wine is matured, stored and, very rarely, shipped. They come in a variety of shapes and sizes, and with local names characteristic of particular areas. They are usually of wood and often of oak.

District	Name	Contents in litres	Contents in cases
Beaujolais	Pièce	212	23
Bordeaux	Barrique	225	25
Burgundy	Pièce	228	25
Rhine	Halbstück	600	68
Alsace	Foudre	1,000	108

Barrel ageing Wines are aged in barrels. During this time the wine clarifies and matures. Sometimes malolactic fermentation takes place at an early stage. Wood is used because it allows small amounts of air to reach the wine. The wood itself imparts character to the wine so the type and age of timber used is important. Wines are often rotated between new and old barrels.

Barrique *(Fr)* One of the many French words for a BARREL.

Baumé *(Fr)* A hydrometer scale for measuring the density and hence the sugar content of grape juice—from this the probable alcohol content of the finished wine can be calculated.

Beerenauslese *(Ger)* The second highest category of German wine which is even rarer and more expensive than Auslese. The grapes are harvested late and only the ripest from each bunch are used so the sugar content of the unfermented juice is high. Under the German wine law of 1971 Beerenauslese must have an Oechsle reading of at least 120°.

Bentonite (Aluminium silicate) A clay used as a fining agent to remove excess protein.

Binning The laying down of bottled wine for ageing. The bottles are stored on their sides do that the wine is in contact with the cork ensuring an airtight seal. Temperature, humidity and other factors are important if the wine is to age well.

Blending See ASSEMBLAGE.

Body The wine's weight in the mouth due to its alcoholic content and other physical components.

Bond de côté (also bonde à côté) The 'bung-over' position in which many wines in barrel are stored. When the bung is at an angle, less wine evaporates, and therefore the practice makes economic sense to many winemakers.

Botrytis cinerea The 'noble rot', a parasitic fungus or mould which attacks grapes. In German it is called Edelfäule and in French pourriture noble. The fungus penetrates the skin of the fruit causing it to wither. As the grape dries the sugar and flavour become concentrated. The wine produced from these grapes is sweet and high in alcohol. Botrytis cinerea is responsible for some of the finest of the world's sweet white wines such as Sauternes, the Beerenauslesen and Trockenbeerenauslesen of the Rhine and Mosel.

Bottling, cold sterile process Bottling under cold sterile conditions is desirable for nearly all wines which are expected to age in the bottle. Other processes such as pasteurization or hot bottling ensure totally sterile wine and are ideal for wines which will be sold and consumed quickly. In the cold sterile process no heat is used, the bottles are sterilized with sulphur dioxide and filled with wine under an inert carbon dioxide atmosphere to prevent recontamination.

Breed A term used to describe a wine which is distinctive and distinguished—these qualities stemming from such factors as the wine's origin, its soil and the winemaker's skill.

Bouquet This term describes the smells given off by a good mature wine once it has been opened. It results from the slow oxidation in the bottle of alcohol and fruit acids into esters and aldehydes. Wines which are high in acids tend to have a more powerful bouquet than those which are lower in acids. Bouquet should not be confused with AROMA.

Bung This is the stopper for the barrel in which wine is aged. It may be of wood, earthenware or glass.

Cap In red winemaking the solid matter of the grapes which floats to the top of the fermenting vessel. It consists of skins, pips and sometimes stalks. This cap or, in French, chapeau, must be broken up so that the skins are kept in contact with the fermenting juice in order that the maximum amount of colour can be extracted. This is achieved by the process called REMONTAGE.

Cask See BARREL.

Cave *(Fr)* A cellar—this can mean a place for storing wine, sometimes though not always underground. It can also refer to the collection of wine which it contains.

Cellar See CAVE.

Cellar master In France called the chef de cave, the cellar master is responsible for the cellar, its contents and their condition.

Centrifuge A spinning device which pushes the particles in a liquid outward from the centre by centrifugal force thus separating out the particles in suspension. It can be used on must or wine.

Cépage *(Fr)* A grape variety. Pinot Noir, Chardonnay or Cabernet Sauvignon are examples of cépages.

Chais A building for storing wine, usually above ground. It should be distinguished from a *cave* or true cellar, although in practice both terms are interchangeable.

Chapeau See CAP.

Chaptalization The process of adding sugar to the must before or during fermentation in order to increase the potential alcoholic content. This practice is forbidden in Italy but is permitted, under very strict controls, for some wines in certain circumstances in Germany and France.

Château *(Fr)* A wine estate—a wine with a château label should be a wine made entirely from grapes grown on that property. Although château-labelling

GLOSSARY

on most wines is a reliable designation of origin and authenticity, some trade marks use the word château without justification.

Château-bottled A wine made and bottled on the estate on which the grapes were grown. The terms mis du château or mis en bouteilles au château are a guarantee that the wine is unblended with wines from other properties, but it is not necessarily a guarantee of quality.

Chef de cave Cellar master.

Chef de culture Manager of the vineyards at a property.

Chromatographic analysis The analysis of substances in a solution by passing it over an absorbing material so that the constituent parts separate into bands of different colours.

Classed growth In French cru classé. A property which has been awarded an official clasification. The Bordeaux Classification of 1855 was developed for the Paris Exposition Universelle of 1855. A committee of Bordeaux wine-brokers worked out a classification based on soil, prestige and price for the wines of Médoc, Sauternes, and one Graves—Haut Brion. Relatively few changes have been made to this general classification.

Climat Burgundian term for a vineyard—equivalent of cru in Bordeaux.

Clodosporium cellare A fungus present in some cellars—said to give a 'sealing wax' tone to wine.

Clone A group of plants which have been produced vegetatively from a single plant.

Clos (Fr) A walled vineyard, or one that was once walled, especially in Burgundy. The word clos may not appear on a wine label unless the vineyard actually exists and produced the wine. The vineyard must also be surrounded by an enclosure, unless the existence of the clos has been recorded for more than 100 years.

Commune (Fr) A township or parish, an administrative unit consisting of a village and the surrounding land. Many commune names are adopted as official APPELLATION CONTRÔLÉE place names in which case the wines produced within the area must be of a similar standard and quality.

Cooperage General term for wooden casks, barrels or vats used for storage in a particular cellar or winery. Also means storage capacity and the repair of these containers.

Côte (Fr) A slope with vineyards. When used to describe a wine it usually, but not always, refers to wine of lesser quality than a clos or a château. It can also be used to describe a whole area i.e. Côte d'Or, Côte de Beaune, Côte de Nuits.

Cru (Fr) The French term for a growth or a crop of grapes. When applied to a vineyard it means the vineyard and the wine it produces. Most classifications of French wine divide the wines and vineyards into crus. The crus classés or classed growths of the Médoc are divided into five categories: premier cru; deuxième cru; troisième cru; quatrième cru and cinquième cru. Below the crus classés are the crus bourgeois. These are divided into the grands bourgeois, which include 18 crus exceptionnels, and bourgeois growths. This system has been adopted with modifications in other areas. Other Bordeaux regions, for example, have only two categories of classification: premier grand cru classé and grand cru classé. It should be remembered that a troisième cru is not a third class wine—it is one of the finest wines.

Cuvage (Fr) Vatting—putting fresh grape juice into fermenting vats after crushing.

Cuve (Fr) Wine vat, tank or cask, especially a large one in which wines are fermented or blended.

Cuvée (Fr) From cuve—a term meaning the contents of a vat, or all the wine made at one time under the same conditions. It may also refer to a particular batch or blend of a blended wine.

Cuvier (Fr) A winery.

Débourbage (Fr) In the making of white wine the practice of delaying the fermentation of the newly pressed juice for a day or so allowing the juice to 'stand' and clarify. The juice can then be drawn off from the coarse sediment. Centrifuges are sometimes used at this stage in modern wineries. The onset of fermentation is postponed by keeping the juice at low temperatures or by treating it with metabisulphite. Fermentation may then be initiated by the introduction of a culture of selected yeasts.

Décuvage (Fr) Devatting—in the making of red wine the fermentation vats must be emptied in order to separate the fermented grape juice from the skins or marc. This occurs at the end of fermentation after the cap of skins has sunk to the bottom of the vat.

Denominazione di Origine Controllata (DOC) (It) The second level of wine established under the 1963 Italian wine laws and broadly equivalent to the French APPELLATION CONTRÔLÉE. It is a guarantee that the wine comes from a specific vineyard and that the vineyard's production is controlled by law. The top level of wine under the 1963 laws is the denominazione di origine controllata e garantita (DOCG); so far only one has been awarded to Brunello di Montalcino.

Domaine (Fr) A single property or estate which can be made up of several separate vineyards.

Edelfäule (Ger) See BOTRYTIS CINEREA.

Egrappage (Fr) The removal of the stalks from grapes before they are pressed or placed in the fermentation vat. Whether the grapes are destemmed or not depends on the type of wine, the region and the traditional practices of the winemaker. The stalks contain tannin which can render the wine harsh bu they also give the wine lasting qualities. Egrappage also allows the wine to attain higher levels of alcohol for the stalks tend to absorb a certain amount of alcohol during fermentation. Originally the stems were removed manually but this operation is now done mechanically in a machine called an 'égrappoir' or destemmer. Egrappage is usually combined with crushing in an 'égrappoir-fouloir' or stemmer-crusher.

Einzellage (Ger) Under the 1971 German wine laws, Enzellage is used to describe a single vineyard with strictly defined boundaries and a legally approved name. Most Einzellagen have evolved from a consolidation of several small vineyards.

Eiswein (Ger) A rare German wine made from the first pressings of frozen grapes. Grapes harvested after a severe frost will be frozen, the less ripe grapes will be frozen solid, the ripe ones will be only partially frozen. The first run of juice will be from the ripest and therefore only partially frozen grapes. It is a very rare and expensive wine. See QUALITÄTSWEIN MIT PRÄDIKAT.

Estate-bottling Virtually the same as château-bottling and a guarantee that the wine is unblended with wines from other properties. It is also to some extent a guarantee of quality, Terms used on the label to indicate estate bottling are: 'mise du domaine', 'mise du propriétaire', 'mis en bouteilles par le propriétaire' and 'mise à la propriété'.

Estery A sweet, fruity smell which results from the slow reaction between the acids in a wine and the alcohol.

Extract Non-volatile, soluble solids which give wine substance, body and depth. In must and sweet wine, sugar forms the major part of the soluble solids but in a dry wine the extract consists of non-sugar solids.

Fat Term used to describe a wine with a full body, high in glycerol and extract.

Fermentation, alcoholic The process by which sugar is converted into alcohol and carbon dioxide by a series of complex chemical reactions between the sugars in the grape juice and zymase, an enzyme carried in the yeast cells. Today the fermentation process is carefully controlled.

Fermentation, malolactic A secondary fermentation during which the rather green, appley malic acid, a fruit acid, is converted into the milder lactic acid and carbon dioxide. This secondary fermentation can take place straight after the alcoholic fermentation, some time later or, in certain conditions, it may proceed at the same time. It is usually considered desirable in red wines and in white wines where the acidity is too high.

Filtration The clarifying of wine prior to bottling by passing it through a filter—there are many kinds of filter. Many German wines are sterile filtered to remove all bacteria so that the wine can be bottled earlier.

Fining The traditional method of clarifying wine. An organic agent such as gelatin, egg white (for fine red wines) or isinglass (for white wines) is added to the wine causing the particles in suspension to coagulate and settle at the bottom of the cask as sediment or lees. Clay products such as bentonite are also used as fining agents. Fining stabilizes the wine and can improve the flavour if, for example, excess tannin is removed. Nowadays it is being replaced by filtration and centrifuging, though fining is still used for the finest wines.

Finish A wine tasting term which describes a wine's end taste. A wine with a good finish has a firm distinctive end and some length on the palate.

Foudre (Fr) A barrel.

Foulage (Fr) The process of lightly crushing the grapes in order to start the juice running. After crushing, grapes for red wine are pumped into the fermentation vats. Crushing and destemming are often combined in one operation in a stemmer-crusher or 'égrappoir-fouloir'.

Free-run wine Also known as vin de goutte, this is the juice which runs off from the crushed grapes before pressing. It is usually of superior quality. The juice extracted by pressing is known as PRESS WINE.

Frost Many of the fine wines of the world are produced at the northern limit of the vine where frost is a hazard. The period of greatest danger is in spring when the buds have just begun to form. A severe frost can destroy most of the vine and affect not only that year's crop but also the following year's vintage. Growers try to minimize frost by putting heating apparatus among the vines or by spraying water over them—the water freezes and protects the vines.

Generic A name which describes a type of wine, for example, sparkling wine, rosé etc. It can also refer to a region, generic Bordeaux or Burgundy, for example. In the USA and Australia, European wines are 'reproduced', and so the names Sauternes, Chablis and Rhine wine appear on the labels. However,

GLOSSARY

the origin of such wines must be clearly stated and their sale is not allowed in EEC countries.

Glycerol A thick, colourless, sweet-tasting chemical, $CH_2(OH)$. $CHOH.CH_2(OH)$. It is an important component of wine.

Goût de terroir A distinctive earthy taste which some wines have and which is related to the soil of the particular vineyard.

Governo *(It)* A winemaking process practised in the Chianti region. Four different kinds of grapes are fermented together. A small proportion of the vintage, about 5 per cent, is put aside before fermentation. These grapes are left to dry, usually on straw trays or hanging in a well-ventilated attic. These raisinated grapes are added to the wine which has already fermented. The dry sweet grapes cause fermentation to start again. This second fermentation proceeds very slowly and gives the wine more body and a higher glycerol content which is ideal for a Chianti Classico intended for ageing.

Grafting In the late 1800s almost all the existing European vineyards were destroyed by the aphid PHYLLOXERA which was introduced accidentally from America. Almost all European wines now come from species of VITIS VINIFERA grafted onto phylloxera-resistant American rootstocks. Grafting involves taking a twig (scion) from the desired variety and inserting it into a notch cut in the stump of the 'stock'.

Grand vin *(Fr)* A 'great wine', it is not a term which is legally defined.

Grape All grapes belong to the genus *vitis*. The most important species for wine production is VITIS VINIFERA of which there are are almost unlimited varieties. Only about 20 varieties, however, are capable of producing really great wine. Different varieties respond well to certain climatic conditions, soil types etc. In the French APPELLATION D'ORIGINE system and the Italian DOC system, the varieties of grape to be grown in a certain area, or even in a vineyard, are strictly controlled. In Germany, where climatic conditions are hard, there has been considerable experimentation with new grape varieties. These are crosses between different varieties of VITIS VINIFERA and may have desirable qualities such as frost resistance or early ripening.

Graves *(Fr)* The word means gravel but is also used to describe several districts of Bordeaux. Gravelly soil provides excellent drainage for vines.

Grêle *(Fr)* Hail. Hail, like frost, is a natural disaster feared by vinegrowers. A heavy hailstorm can destroy a crop in minutes and, because it is so localized, it may destroy one vineyard whilst the neighbouring vineyard is unaffected. Hail breaks the skin of the fruit and the leaves rendering them susceptible to attack by disease. Even a light hail can bruise berries giving wine, especially red wine, a 'goût de grêle', a faint taste of rot in the wine. Growers sometimes attempt to encourage hail to fall as rain by dispersing clouds with light aircraft. Occasionally nets are put over vines as protection against hail.

Grey rot In French pourriture grise— a disease caused by the same fungus, BOTRYTIS CINEREA, which causes noble rot. Only when conditions of high humidity are followed by hot weather does pourriture grise become pourriture noble, and this is only desirable on certain varieties of white grapes such as Riesling and Sémillon.

Grosslage *(Ger)* A large vineyard. Under the 1971 German wine law, it denotes a vineyard name which extends over several wine producing areas.

Hybrid This is the result of a cross between American and European vines. This is done in order to try to combine the best qualities of the parent plant or to produce an offspring which can contend with problems such as frost or phylloxera. Most French hybrids bear the name of the hybridizer and a number—for example Baco No. 1, Seibel 13053, Seyve-Villard 5/247. In France these hybrids are banned from all AC areas. There is a fundamental difference between a 'crossing' of two *vitis vinifera* grape varieties and a hybrid or 'producteur direct'.

Inoculation A term used to describe the introduction of a special yeast culture into the must. This is usually done after all the wild yeasts have been destroyed by sulphur dioxide.

Isinglass Purified fish glue—the most common fining agent for white wines.

Kabinett *(Ger)* The lowest of the Qualitätswein mit Prädikat divisions under the 1971 German wine law. It ranks just under Spätlese in quality.

Kellermeister *(Ger)* Cellar master.

Late picked Some grapes, such as Riesling, can be left on the vine after the main vintage. They will obviously be at the mercy of the weather, but the extra time on the vine allows the grapes to accumulate sugar. In Germany these late picked grapes are called Spätlese and in France vendange tardive. In Germany selected bunches are chosen for late harvesting—a process known as Auslese. Single grapes from a bunch may also be selected for the Beerenauslese, and, last of all, overripe grapes which have been attacked by BOTRYTIS CINEREA or Edelfäule may be selected to make the rarest and sweetest of German wines—the Trockenbeerenauslese.

Lees The heavy coarse sediment containing dead yeasts which is left in the barrel when young wine is racked off into other barrels.

Loess A fine fertile soil based on wind-blown dust—a mixture of loam, lime, sand and mica.

Maceration The process of extracting flavour and colour from grapes by steeping them in their own liquid before fermentation.

Malic acid One of the fruit acids—it is particularly tart. It is converted by a secondary fermentation known as MALOLACTIC FERMENTATION into lactic acid and carbon dioxide. This reduces the acid taste of the wine.

Marc *(Fr)* The solid matter consisting of skins, stalks and seeds which is left after the wine (red wine) or juice (white wine) has been extracted by pressing. It is also called pomace.

Must Grape juice or crushed grapes before fermentation.

Négociant *(Fr)* A wine merchant or shipper who buys in wine from growers and prepares it for sale.

Noble rot See BOTRYTIS CINEREA.

Nose Term for a wine's bouquet or aroma.

Oechsle *(Ger)* Hydrometer scale for measuring the sugar content of must of grape juice before fermentation. From this the future alcoholic content of the wine can be calculated.

Oeonologist A trained graduate of oenology, which is the science of wine, its production, care and handling.

Off-taste A rather broad wine tasting term to describe a wine which has an abnormal taste, for whatever reason. It usually denotes unhealthy wine.

Oidium One of the many diseases to which vines are prone, it is caused by a fungus which attacks the leaves, shoots and tendrils. It is now controlled by spraying with a sulphur solution.

Phylloxera A disease of vines caused by the aphid *phylloxera vastatrix*. It was accidentally introduced to Europe from America in about 1860. By the end of the century it had destroyed most European vineyards. Unfortunately, VITIS VINIFERA, from which most of the world's best wines are made, is particularly prone to its depredations. American vines which have tougher roots are resistant to phylloxera and most European vines are now grafted onto American stocks.

Pièces See BARREL.

Piges Wooden poles used to keep the CAP of skins submerged in the fermenting must.

Pomace Mass of skins, seeds and stems left in the press after the wine or juice has been drawn off. The French term is MARC.

Pourriture noble See BOTRYTIS CINEREA.

Pouriture vulgaire See GREY ROT.

Pressing In red winemaking the skins are fermented with the juice, the wine is drawn off and the skins are then pressed. In the vinification of white wine, however, the juice is fermented without the skins so pressing occurs beforehand. There are several kinds of press in commercial use. The vertical hydraulic press (now rarely found) incoporates a cylinder, pressing the skins against a metal disc above. The wine runs through the sides of the cylinder into a vat below. The horizontal press consists of a long horizontal wooden cylinder which holds the grapes. This cylinder is rotated and the two ends move slowly towards the centre exerting a slow but even pressure on the grapes. It is important that the pressure is not great enough to break open the pips. There is another horizontal press, the pneumatic press, which gives a gentle pressing by means of a rubber 'bladder' in the centre which swells, pressing the grapes against the sides.

Press wine Also called vin de presse, this is the wine extracted by pressing the MARC after the free-run wine is drawn off. It is inclined to be hard and is sometimes mixed with vin de goutte in varying proportions to add body.

Qualitätswein bestimmter Anbaugebiete (QbA) *(Ger)* Wine which must come from a certain area and from particular grape varieties. It must have an Oechsle reading of 65° and have an official registration number on the bottle. Unlike the QUALITÄTSWEIN MIT PRÄDIKAT wines, it may be chaptalized.

Qualitätswein mit Prädikat (QmP) *(Ger)* The highest category of German wine under the 1971 wine law. The five predicates are: Kabinett, Spätlese, Auslese, Beerenauslese and Trockenbeerenauslese. All the wines in these five categories must be made from unsugared musts. All QmP wine will have a registration number printed on the label.

Racking The drawing off of wine from one vat or barrel to another leaving behind the sediment or lees. This process is called soutirage in French, Abstich in German and travaso in Italian. Good wines are normally racked between two and six times before bottling. Racking usually follows fining. White wines are more delicate than red and are usually racked fewer times to avoid oxidation.

Remontage Removing a portion of the must from the bottom of the fermentation vat and pumping it over the top. This keeps the cap submerged and in contact with the fermenting must.

Riserva *(It)* Reserve—a word often found on wine labels which has a legal

GLOSSARY

standing in Italian DOC law.

Rootstock See GRAFTING.

Rotation The growing of different crops in a regular order to avoid soil exhaustion—a practice not often used in vineyards nowadays. Wine can also be rotated between new and older casks.

Sediment A deposit of solids and possibly crystals which accumulate in some wines as they age in bottle. Red wines deposit more sediment than white—it is composed of TANNIN, pigment and small quantities of mineral salts. The sediment in white wine usually consists of colourless crystals of cream of tartar—these are tasteless, harmless and will often disappear if the wine is left for some time at room temperature. Sediment is not a defect, and, indeed, indicates that a wine has not been over treated. It should be left in the bottle when the wine is poured.

Spätlese *(Ger)* The second of the QUALITÄTSWEIN MIT PRÄDIKAT categories above Kabinett in quality and below Auslese. It is made from late picked grapes and must have an Oechsle reading of 85°.

Stalks Stalks are sometimes added to the fermenting wine to give it extra 'backbone'. They are high in acid and may make the wine disagreeably astringent. They also tend to remove colour and alcohol. Whether they are added depends on the vintage and the traditional practice of the winemaker. The French term for destemming is égrappage.

Stemmer-crusher A rotating cylindrical machine which removes the stalks and lightly crushes the grapes.

Sulphiting Sulphur in the form of sulphuric acid, sulphur dioxide or sulphites is sometimes added to grape juice or must in order to delay or prevent fermentation. This is common practice in modern wineries in which a culture of a selected yeast is added later.

Sulphurizing The sterilizing of barrels and casks and also the treatment of vines in the field to safeguard against OIDIUM. Sulphur is a disinfectant.

Süssreserve *(Ger)* Concentrated unfermented grape must which is kept back in order to be added to the wine just before bottling. This sweetens and softens the wine. The process which is allowed up to Spätlese is called Süssung. However, the Süssreserve must come from the same category of wine, for example, the Süssreserve for Spätlese must come from Spätlese juice, and from the same vineyard or district.

Tafelwein *(Ger)* Table wine—under the 1971 wine laws it ranks below QUALITÄTSWEIN in quality. It will always be sugared and will never carry the name of a vineyard.

Tannin A group of organic compounds found in wine—they are also found in the wood, bark, roots and stems of many plants. It is astringent to taste, making the mouth pucker. It is particularly pronounced in wines which have not had their stems removed before fermentation. Additional tannin may be picked up from the oak barrels in which wine is stored, especially from new barrels.

Tartaric acid The principal acid of wine made from ripe grapes. It is usually precipitated in the form of crystals of potassium bitartrate in the cask or in the bottle. This can be avoided by cold treatment before bottling. However, the crystals are harmless and do not detract from the wine's quality.

Tastevin This is a flat, shallow, silver winetaster's cup, used traditionally in Burgundy for judging new wine. When a wine is 'tastevine', it is approved by the Confrérie des Chevaliers du Tastevin and carries a special label. This applies only in Burgundy.

Tirage *(Fr)* A bottling. Several casks are usually assembled in a vat for a 'tirage' or bottling.

Topping up The filling up of casks or barrels of young wine with similar quality wine. It is usually carried out weekly to ensure that there is no air space or ullage between the wine and the bung. This prevents oxidation of the wine.

Trockenbeerenauslese *(Ger)* The top of the five QUALITÄTSWEIN predicated wines. The grapes are harvested very late and the berries are individually selected from the vine. Only those which have been attacked by BOTRYTIS CINEREA or Edelfäule will be used, ensuring that the wine will be very sweet.

Varietals Wines, especially American wines, which take their name from the name of the grape rather than from their place of origin. Under American law only a wine which has at least 51 per cent of a particular grape in it can take its name from that grape. However, fine wines from top wineries contain 100 per cent of the grape variety on the label.

Vat A large vessel in which wine is fermented or stored. Traditionally they were made of wood, but these days they may be of glass, enamel-lined concrete, or stainless steel.

Vin de goutte See FREE RUN WINE.

Vin de press See PRESS WINE.

Vintage The annual grape harvest and the wine made from those grapes. It has come to mean a wine year, thus, 1978 is a good vintage in Bordeaux and Burgundy.

Vitis vinifera The family of grape varieties from which almost all good European wines are made. Originally it came from the Middle East. Its great disadvantage is that it is susceptible to PHYLLOXERA, a problem overcome by grafting onto phylloxera-resistant rootstocks from America.

Yeasts Unicellular organisms some of which—saccharomyces elipsoideus—bring about fermentation in grapae juice. It is the zymase in the yeasts which actually catalyses the fermentation process and turns the grape juice into wine. There are many different yeast cultures suitable for particular conditions.

INDEX

INDEX